"A must read for coaches at all levels."
—Anson Dorrance, Head Soccer Coach,
UNC, 16-time national champions

"The audience at our annual alumnae conference was mesmerized and enlightened when Michael Gelb introduced them to the juggling metaphor. Reading this book will have the same effect on you!"
—Karen Page, Chair, Harvard Business School Alumnae Association and James Beard Award-winning author

"Michael Gelb taught me how to juggle in 1975. He introduced me to a profound metaphor for accelerating the learning process, which I have applied in my own life and work ever since. This amazing book is like a series of private lessons with Gelb: Reading it will enrich your life and make you smile inside."
—Tony Buzan, author of *The Mind Map Book*

"Michael Gelb's playful, relaxed 'mistake-positive' approach to learning and change unleashed in me a delightful sense of freedom and courage. Gelb emphasizes that great coaches guide people to realize that they are capable of more than they might have imagined. That's the effect this book will have on you! *More Balls Than Hands* will bring your organization back to life and your life back to joy."
—Marcia Reynolds, author of *How to Outsmart Your Brain* and Past President of International Coaches Federation

"In a world of hyperchange, rapid adaptation—the ability to learn something new and apply it quickly and effectively—is the most important and most accessible source of sustainable competitive advantage. *More Balls Than Hands* is a scintillating, serious resource for gaining this advantage."
—Professor Jim Clawson, Darden Graduate Business School

More Balls
Than Hands

Prentice
Hall Press

More Balls
Than Hands

*Juggling Your Way to Success
by Learning to Love Your Mistakes*

Michael J. Gelb

PRENTICE HALL

Published by the Penguin Group

Penguin Group (USA) Inc., 375 Hudson Street, New York, New York 10014, U.S.A.

Penguin Books Ltd, 80 Strand, London WC2R 0RL, England

Penguin Books Australia Ltd, 250 Camberwell Road, Camberwell, Victoria 3124, Australia

Penguin Books Canada Ltd, 10 Alcorn Avenue, Toronto, Ontario, Canada M4V 3B2

Penguin Books India (P) Ltd, 11 Community Centre, Panchsheel Park, New Delhi – 110 017, India

Penguin Books (N.Z.) Ltd, Cnr Rosedale and Airborne Roads, Albany, Auckland, New Zealand

Penguin Books (South Africa) (Pty) Ltd, 24 Sturdee Avenue,

Rosebank, Johannesburg 2196, South Africa

Penguin Books Ltd, Registered Offices:

80 Strand, London WC2R 0RL, England

First published in 2003 by Prentice Hall,

a member of Penguin Group (USA) Inc.

1 3 5 7 9 10 8 6 4 2

Library of Congress Cataloging-in-Publication Data

Gelb, Michael.

More balls than hands : juggling your way to success by learning to love your mistakes /
Michael J. Gelb.

p. cm.

Includes index.

ISBN 0-7352-0337-7

1. Success—Psychological aspects. 2. Success in business. I. Title.

BF637.S8G39 2003

158.1—dc21   2003051720

This book is printed on acid-free paper. ∞

Printed in the United States of America

Set in Garamond Book

Designed by Erin Benach

To the maestro of balance,
Dr. Mort Herskowitz

"I fall down. I get up. I keep on dancing."

—ancient Jewish wisdom

FOREWORD BY TONY SCHWARTZ

Michael Gelb is a man of infinite energy, bursting creativity, and huge enthusiasm for life. He is a model, in short, of everything he celebrates, which is rare in itself. To understand what accounts for the highest levels of excellence and how to achieve them, Michael works from at least two angles. The first is to meticulously study the work of great geniuses.

Michael did this to inspiring effect in *How to Think Like Leonardo da Vinci,* choosing as his subject one of history's most eclectically creative geniuses. To deconstruct the secret of da Vinci's towering accomplishments, Michael extracted seven accessible principles that defined it—among them such unlikely ones as the willingness to embrace paradox and ambiguity, the cultivation of physical grace, and the appreciation for the interconnectedness of all things.

Da Vinci only fired Michael's curiosity and he went on, in *Discover Your Genius,* to write about what we all stand to learn from the unique talents of other great geniuses such as Plato, Brunelleschi, Columbus, Copernicus, Elizabeth I, Shakespeare, Jefferson, Gandhi, and Einstein. In accessible language, he helps pull from these geniuses the particular lessons we mortals can use in our everyday lives.

The second way that Michael seeks to understand more about learning and excellence is by pursuing both himself. Along the way, he has developed a dazzling array of skills. He is a black belt in Aikido, a master teacher of the Alexander Technique, and a wonderful chef. He has also been a juggler for the past twenty-five years.

What interests Michael, above all, is learning, and more specifically, how to learn. The book you now hold is about just that, and specifically about how learning to juggle has all kinds of applications to achieving success individually and organizationally. Juggling is a particularly appealing metaphor for these times. The reality is that most of us are compelled to juggle many more balls every day than we have hands to hold them. Our challenge is to keep as many balls as possible in the air, as delicate a task as that often is. There is something wonderful about the fact that juggling teaches us quite literally to become more balanced and poised.

Michael takes these ideas a step further, indeed several steps further. He finds in juggling a series of apt connections to qualities and skills that we need to succeed in our work, among them relaxed concentration, persistence, visualization, and, above all, the willingness to fail. I resonate with these insights, because they are well documented in the work that my own partners and I have done with world-class athletes over the years, helping them to perform better under pressure.

The notion of learning to love our mistakes may be antithetical to the culture we live in, but it is also wonderfully freeing and intuitively on point. Dropping the balls in the course of learning to juggle, Michael argues persuasively, is an ideal way to learn how to cope with mistakes gracefully. He goes on to ask the provocative question "What would it be like if you could view your mistakes with affection?"

The ability to learn and grow is closely tied to our willingness to take risks and to make mistakes along the way. As Michael points out, we need only watch infants, who learn at an amazing pace, to realize that failure is built into success. By contrast, the fear of failure is the primary impediment that we all face in learning, and this fear undermines both individual and organizational performance in the face of constantly changing demands.

Imagine, however, that none of these sorts of metaphors move you much—that you are the sort of person who is interested only in what juggling (and learning to juggle) can do for you directly in your everyday life. There's good news here too. If juggling did nothing else for you, it is a terrific way to build play into the course of your working day. As every great athlete understands, intermittent recovery and renewal are critical to sustained performance. Juggling, even a few minutes at a time in the midst of an otherwise pressing schedule, is a terrific way to shift gears physically, emotionally, and mentally. Indeed, juggling prompts a shift from the ordinary analytic left hemisphere mode of the brain to the more imaginative right hemisphere mode.

Whether it's to become better at work or at play—or to recognize the close connection between the two—the wisdom contained in this book is a route to more success and satisfaction in whatever you set out to achieve.

ACKNOWLEDGMENTS

I'm grateful to the wonderful people who contributed to the creation of this book. Special thanks to:

My juggling teachers, partners, and buddies, including Dennis Masella, Stuart Haber, Kit Summers, Tony Duncan, and Lloyd "Tim" Timberlake;

Alexander Technique teachers and colleagues, especially Walter Carrington, Paul Collins, Beret Arcaya, Frank Ottiwell, Gwen Ellison, Stacy Forsythe, Michael Frederick, Barbara Kent, and Betty Rajna;

Aikido masters Dr. Clyde Takeguchi, Harvey Konigsberg, Yoshimitsu Yamada, and Mitsugi Saotome;

Learning guides J. G. Bennett and Dr. Mort Herskowitz;

Clients and friends who apply the juggling metaphor method in leading their organizations, especially Ed Basset, Mitch Becker, Edward Cardimona, Marti Chaney, David Chu, Delano Lewis, Marv Damsma, Debbie Benami-Rahm, Dennis McIntosh, Dr. Tom Jenkins, Tom Quick, Campbell Gerrish, Ketan Patel, Gerry Kirk, and Jim Sutton;

Penguin Putnam editors Adrian Zackheim and Stephanie Land; jacket designer Joseph Perez; publicists Will Weisser and Allison Sweet; and copy editor Emily DeHuff.

Rowan Frederick was my wonderful illustrator.

Muriel Nellis and her staff, especially Jane Roberts;

Office administrator and rock of support Mary Hogan;

Friends who offered valuable feedback and support: Susan Greenberg, Ernie Tremblay, Barbara Horowitz, Dr. Marvin Hyett, Nina Lesavoy, Karen Lee, Karen Page, David Kendall, Dr. Allison Rossett, Dr. Ruth Clark, Tony Schwartz, Jennifer Spoelker, Dr. Jodie Katz, Lorie Dechar, Ron Gross, Dean Sluyter, Susan RoAne, Marcia Weider, Rowan

Acknowledgments

Frederick, Greg Brittenham, Anson Dorrance, Giovanna d'Alessio, Grandmaster Raymond Keene, O.B.E., Dr. Dale Schusterman, Mark Levy, Sandy and Joan Gelb.

And extra-special thanks to Tony Buzan, for inventing Mind Maps—the supreme method for juggling with ideas.

CONTENTS

Contents

LIST OF ILLUSTRATIONS

INTRODUCTION: FROM THE TIP OF MICK JAGGER'S TONGUE TO THE LEARNING ORGANIZATION

I'm standing on the tip of Mick Jagger's tongue juggling a rubber chicken, a turnip, and a big pointy kitchen fork in front of 250,000 people. No, it's not a "bad trip" or a weird dream; it's the Knebworth Rock Festival in 1977, and my juggling partner Lloyd "Tim" Timberlake (former science editor for Reuters) and I are performing between Rolling Stones sets on a giant stage shaped like Mick Jagger's mouth. Tim was also juggling a chicken, turnip, and fork, and our big-finish trick involved tossing the turnip high in the air and catching it on the tip of the fork while making chicken noises. In full cluck, the turnips flew high as we raised our forks in unison and . . . we both missed! We discovered immediately that there's something liberating about being laughed at by a quarter of a million people. A couple of helpful, or perhaps sadistic, audience members tossed the errant turnips back to us and we tried again. This time it worked. The vast ocean of denim and hair before us exploded in cheers followed by a powerful chant: "Bring on the Stones, bring on the Stones!"

Tim and I were lucky—we knew how to embrace our mistakes and were able to turn our near-disastrous performance on stage into a huge success. But I had an opportunity not too long afterward to witness how fear of mistakes and of change could sabotage one's performance, especially in the workplace. Later that year I was invited to present at a five-day senior management retreat for Digital Equipment Corporation (a friend had recommended me to Digital because of my research into accelerated learning and creative thinking). DEC was growing rapidly and introducing a "matrixed" organizational structure. The vice-presidential team was charged with implementing this new structure and leading the company through dramatic changes. But even in an organization born at the dawn of the dynamic "information age," resistance to learning and change was a major problem. People at all levels had trouble acknowledging and taking responsibility for mistakes. Because the company was growing so quickly, most managers felt that they were being asked to accomplish more with inadequate resources. (This also happens when there are cutbacks.) Despite the new "matrix," territoriality and internal competition were often stronger forces than teamwork and cooperation. And many talented technical people were promoted to senior management positions on the basis of their technical accomplishments rather than their leadership and communication skills.

In one-on-one conversations, team members confided that they frequently felt overwhelmed. Some of the representative comments included:

- "I work six fourteen-hour days a week but never get through my in-box."
- "Work devours all my time. My life is out of balance. I'm afraid I'm neglecting my family, not to mention my health."
- "As soon as I feel as if I've got firm footing, somebody pulls the rug out from under me."
- "I've got multiple projects and not enough time to attend to them, but there are serious negative consequences for inattention, both personally and professionally."

One manager summed it all up by saying:

"I've got too much to juggle!"

In the course of that five-day session, all of the managers actually learned how to juggle; more importantly, they learned how to use the metaphor of juggling to **overcome resistance to learning and change**. They also gained inspiring, practical insights into teamwork, coaching skills, and the secret of getting more done with fewer resources.

Since that initial session in 1977, people have only become more stressed, more pressed for time, and more desperate to find a way to make changes in their lives that will help them find the balance they seek. The juggling metaphor has never been so apt. The March 25, 2002, edition of *Newsweek* featured a story on Google founders Larry Page and Sergy Brin that highlighted their ability to balance their company's growth in the heyday of the Internet boom with a sound approach to maintaining profitability and cash flow. The story includes a photograph of Brin standing next to a unicycle while juggling three balls in his office. For many years, the women's magazine *Redbook* aimed its advertising to appeal to "The Redbook Juggler," the woman struggling to balance concerns about family, health, career, finances, and personal growth. The featured story in the February 9, 2003, edition of the *New York Times Week in Review* was entitled "Juggler-in-Chief" and featured an illustration of a figure standing behind a presidential podium juggling six balls. The article chronicled the challenge for presidents throughout history to balance multiple crises. Whether managing a country, a company, or an individual life, the metaphor of juggling speaks to all of us as a reminder of the importance of balance.

Over the past twenty-five years, I have refined the metaphor and used juggling to help thousands of people let go of their stress in exchange for a new enthusiasm for learning and change. Companies such as AMEC, British Petroleum, Compaq (which acquired DEC before being acquired by HP), DuPont, KPMG, IBM, Merck, Microsoft, Nike, and many others have successfully applied juggling in their organizational development efforts after attending my High Performance Learning workshop. *More Balls Than Hands* offers you everything I teach in my workshop and more. In the pages that follow you'll be guided through the practical application of these ideas to some of your most pressing organizational and personal challenges.

More Balls Than Hands is based on the research-validated assumptions that your learning potential is virtually unlimited and that your learning ability can improve with age. Learning how to capitalize on your learning power, and how to help others do the same, is an essential component of leadership that can be developed. This book is for leaders who aim to promote high performance by creating a culture that supports and rewards rapid, continuous learning and improvement (a **learning organization**) and who also want to live balanced, fulfilling lives as they take on more responsibility.

In addition to its applications in the workplace, you will be delighted to discover that you can apply the juggling metaphor to raise your confidence, enthusiasm, and ability to learn anything. These ideas can provide the missing link in improving your performance in golf, skiing, tennis, or any other sport. If you are a parent, you'll be able to apply what you'll learn to accelerate your children's progress in learning and life. And, as a bonus, you may even learn how to juggle.

The Learning Organization

> In an uncertain world, where all we know for sure is that nothing is sure, we are going to need organizations that are continually renewing themselves, reinventing themselves, reinvigorating themselves. These are the learning organizations, the ones with the learning habit.
>
> Without that habit of learning, they will not dream the dream, let alone have any hope of managing it.
>
> —Charles Handy,
> *Managing the Dream*

Susan Greenberg designs and coordinates the training program for content designers and developers in the Microsoft Training and Certification group. Greenberg comments, "Our people are the best, highly motivated, and very talented, but nevertheless they sometimes resist change and have a fear of the unknown. The juggling metaphor is a perfect tool for facilitating openness to new learning. It helps us create a playful, exploratory environment and makes it easier for our developers to be willing to "drop the balls" in order to learn new tricks!"

Ketan Patel is a managing director at Goldman Sachs. He leads a team of gifted strategists who provide consultation, analysis, and advice for clients at high levels in government and industry globally. In the past few years Patel has been able to elevate a number of his people to more significant roles. He comments on what differentiates the people he's been able to promote: "All of them are brilliant, top-of-the-class types, but the ones who make it are those who embrace the challenge of learning something new without being shackled by the fear of failure. If they're already juggling three balls and I toss them a flaming stick, they seem to know which ball to toss to another team member in order to catch the stick and keep on juggling."

Jim Sutton is the head of human resources for a division of Nike, a company that attracts high-energy, highly competitive people. Jim observes that "our company is filled with achievers and winners in sales, manufacturing, marketing, and design, but being a great sales person or designer doesn't necessarily make you a great head of sales or design. The skills of managing, coaching, teaching, listening, facilitating, and coordinating (rather than competing with other internal groups) are at a premium. We are always looking for ways to help our leaders keep all these balls in the air!"

Susan, Ketan, and Jim are all leaders in developing learning organizations. And they know that a successful learning organization must be staffed and led by people who know how to learn. Years ago, Peter Drucker wrote that the manager of the future will be a "learning guide." That future is now.

Continuous Learning: The Champion's Spirit

Leadership authorities such as Peter Drucker, Jim Clawson, Peter Senge, Stephen Covey, and Warren Bennis all agree that the commitment to rapid, continuous learning is an essential element of individual and organizational high performance. That commitment was alive at a recent World Juggling Championship event. The competitors amazed the audience of more than two thousand people by performing mind-boggling variations with up to seven balls. All of the competitors dropped the balls during the course of their acts. Yet each recovered quickly and continued without missing a beat. Why did the world's best jugglers all make mistakes? Because they were all attempting to push the limits of the possible. The ultimate winner was Tony Duncan, a professional juggler from Brooklyn, who thrilled the crowd with an astonishing original performance. The next day, the sponsoring organization offered a seminar on the principles contained in this book. Who was first in line? That's right, it was Tony Duncan, the world champion. He said, "I'm hoping that I can learn something from this that will help me get just a little bit better."

"From One Thing, Know Ten Thousand"

In the 1980s, Samurai sword master Miyamoto Musashi's classic *The Book of Five Rings* was translated into English and became an instant business best-seller. Musashi's masterpiece remains a valuable guide for strategists in an increasingly complex world. Musashi emphasized "From one thing, know ten thousand." In other words, learn to think metaphorically—in his case, to extrapolate the principles of swordsmanship to business and life in general. Today—though life and death combat remains a compelling metaphor for business—

economies, supply chains, funding sources, and communications have become so interdependent that a new paradigm of business is emerging which emphasizes cooperation and collaboration in balance with competition. Now juggling provides a marvelous, more appropriate metaphor for this evolving model.

Why? Because learning anything involves keeping a number of things "up in the air" at the same time; because "dropping the balls" provides an ideal way to communicate the importance of coping with mistakes gracefully, one of life's most important abilities. Juggling also promotes a sense of inner quiet and resourcefulness in the midst of activity, a special experience of mind and body in harmony. And juggling's essential lightheartedness encourages easy access to the fundamental human learning modality of play.

Juggling is surprisingly easy to learn and offers equal opportunity to both genders and to people of all ages. You can do it on your own or with others, and all you need to begin is more balls than hands. Progress in juggling is easy to measure and you can continue improving throughout your life. And it's just plain fun.

Management: It's a Lot Like Juggling

Professor James Clawson of the University of Virginia's Darden Graduate Business School notes that the most effective managers are a lot like jugglers. He comments: "Over the years, I've observed two dominant ways of trying to work: the Project Finishers and the Time Allocators. Project Finishers try to focus their efforts and get a thing done before moving on to the next thing. They are thorough and effective, but they can handle only one ball at a time. They make good researchers and doers, but they usually can't manage their way out of a wet paper bag. Time Allocators, on the other hand, do not organize their work by projects, but rather by short allotments of time spread across a wide variety of tasks including meetings, phone calls, interviews, and a myriad of other short activities. They are much more effective in management positions.

"The Time-Allocation approach to work seems very much like juggling. How does one keep multiple balls in the air? And how do we discover the optimum number that can be succesfully managed? If there are too many balls, they all fall. If there are too few, not as much gets done. The principles of juggling seem to help: Develop a stable, reliable process for handling one project or item (focus on the throw), and then apply that process to other projects. Keep all of the items in 'sight' without paying too much attention to any one (soft eyes). A touch here, a note there, an encouragement there— all keep the balls in the air. Time Allocators develop a rhythm, an inner sense of how much time it takes to keep a project from falling to the floor. Like the juggler, the Time Allocator handles projects lightly but firmly and with a familiar repetition that makes the result more effective than he might have a right to expect. The ultimate result can be both mesmerizing and quite remarkable. The best managers are indeed jugglers—their projects are their juggling balls. Like jugglers, the faster and the better managers learn how to handle first one, then two, then three, then four projects with an easy, rhythmic, repeating pattern, the more effective they become."

 Becoming an Ambidextrous Leader

"Balance your brain, balance your body. The future lies with the ambidextrous human!"
—Professor Raymond Dart

Many people excuse themselves from dancing by claiming to have "two left feet" or from juggling by protesting that they have "two left hands." But what if you had two right hands? That's the literal meaning of ambidexterity ("ambi" means "both"; dexterity—from "right-handed"—the ability to perform). Some people are born with the ability to use both hands equally well. Studies by Dr. Frederick Leboyer and others show, for example, that children born in the most supportive, natural environments have a 24 percent higher incidence of natural ambidexterity.

But you don't have to be born ambidextrous to achieve a greater balance between left and right. It's a skill you can cultivate. And because the left side of your cerebral cortex controls the right side of your body and vice versa, many researchers speculate that physical and mental ambidexterity may be related.

Professor Raymond Dart was one of the most notable researchers to offer this opinion. Renowned as one of history's great anatomists and anthropologists, Professor Dart is most famous for his discovery of the remains of *Australopithecus africanus*. When I asked him in an interview in 1980 to summarize his lifetime of study of human nature and the implications for the development of human potential, Dart exclaimed: "Balance your brain, balance your body. The future lies with the ambidextrous human!"

In the same interview, Professor Dart heartily endorsed juggling as a training device to encourage this naturally poised human state. He enthusiastically supported the notion that juggling promotes rhythmic coordination between the two sides of the body and the two sides of the brain. And he emphasized that a balanced body tends to promote a more balanced brain, and vice versa.

Observations of superior performance in a variety of human activities show a high percentage of ambidextrous individuals. Leonardo da Vinci and Michelangelo, for example, both cultivated their ambidexterity. Michelangelo regularly amazed his students and other observers by switching hands while sculpting his masterpieces. And da Vinci's ambidextrous efforts included drawing, painting, and writing with either hand as well as juggling at the court of his patron Ludovico Sforza, Duke of Milan.

In sports, many of the all-time great athletes are ambidextrous. Examples include boxing champions Jack Dempsey, Joe Louis, Sugar Ray Robinson, Muhammad Ali, and Julio Cesar Chavez; baseball stars Mickey Mantle and Eddie Murray; and basketball greats Larry Bird, Magic Johnson, and Michael Jordan.

The metaphor of ambidexterity offers an important key to high performance in business, too. Professor John Kotter of Harvard Business School has spent decades profiling the most effective executives in the business world and has concluded that the very best are those who balance the skills of leadership (envisioning, inspiring, guiding change) with the skills of management (measuring, controlling, implementing). Deborah Tannen, author of *You Just Don't Understand* and many other books on the differences between male and female communication styles, suggests that the very best leaders are able to apply both styles in balance. Brain researcher Ned Hermann has developed a leadership model based on patterns of hemispheric dominance. He concludes that the most effective leaders are those who find a harmonious balance between left (logic, analysis) and right (imagination, intuition) cortical functions. Juggling is a simple, delightful way to remember and communicate the importance of balance between leadership and management, male and female communication styles, left and right hemispheres. As award-winning author and coordinator of the Harvard Business School Women's Alumnae Association Karen Page comments: "When it comes to finding balance in our crazy world, we all need all the help we can get. Learning to juggle, which had always seemed impossible to me, was not only a tremendous boost for my confidence in my ability to learn anything, but it also serves as a kind of daily meditation on balance and a reminder to think both/and instead of either/or."

 Embracing Change

Organizational learning begins with individual learning, and effective organizational change begins with individuals who are committed to the change.

Resistance to change is a common problem, and many light bulbs

> How many leadership gurus,
> management consultants,
> and executive coaches does
> it take to change a light bulb?
>
> Only one, but the light bulb has to
> want to change!

want to stay comfortably screwed in. Since accelerating change is now an unavoidable part of our lives, it makes sense to learn how to give it a positive twist. We can gain valuable perspective by considering the stories of people who have risen to the challenge of change against great adversity.

In his marvelous book *It's Not About the Bike,* Lance Armstrong offers an inspiring example of this resilient, positive approach to embracing change. Describing the lessons learned from his successful battle to overcome cancer and regain his status as the world's greatest long-distance cyclist, Armstrong writes, "The truth is, if you asked me to choose between winning the Tour de France and cancer, I would choose cancer. Odd as it sounds, I would rather have the title of cancer survivor than winner of the Tour because of what it has done for me as a human being, a man, a husband, a son, and a father. . . . My winning the Tour was a symbolic act, proof that you can not only survive cancer, but thrive after it. Maybe, as my friend Phil Knight says, I am hope."

Juggler Kit Summers provides another uplifting example of a hopeful, winning attitude in the face of sudden and catastrophic change. In 1977 he placed first in a nationally televised talent show. He set a world record by juggling seven clubs thirty times and in 1979 became the juggling coach for the Ringling Brothers circus. By 1982 he was starring on stage at a major casino. And then, while crossing the street on the way to work, he was hit by a truck. After thirty-seven days in a coma he awoke to discover that he couldn't walk, talk, or feed himself, and, worst of all, he couldn't juggle. With patience, hope, and discipline, Kit set out on the arduous road to recovery. On the first anniversary of his accident, Kit performed in public, and although his skill hadn't quite returned to its previous level, he was on his way to regaining his stature as one of the best jugglers in the world. Kit has also become a world-class motivational speaker and a successful author. His secrets? Total commitment to learning and change, a positive attitude toward setbacks, strong models of excellence, a supportive community of friends and fellow jugglers, and step-by-step goal setting.

In every dramatic story of surviving and thriving against the odds, one factor remains consistent: a profound commitment to embracing change. But don't wait until you get hit by a truck or become ill to change the things that prevent you from living your life to the fullest. Celebrate being alive every day. Live your highest aspirations, begin learning what you have always wanted to learn.

Becoming *Better* at Learning as You Get Older

> "No matter how old you may be at this moment, it's never too late to change your brain for the better. That's because the brain is different from every other organ in our body. While the liver and lungs and kidneys wear out after a certain number of years, the brain gets sharper the more it's used. Indeed it improves with use."
>
> —Dr. Richard Restak,
> brain researcher

"I'll never be able to do this!" I hear this a lot during my seminars as I put three balls in participants' hands for the first time. Unfortunately, these people often have the same attitude in approaching organizational challenges. Managers frequently ask for help in getting people to "be more open to change" and "think outside the box" and comment that staff members are "set in their ways" and "locked in their 'stovepipes' or 'silos.'"

Moreover, many people assume that our mental and physical abilities inevitably decline with age—that we are, after age twenty-five, losing significant brain capacity on a daily basis. But full appreciation of your remarkable birthright to virtually unlimited learning power comes when you understand that **your brain is designed to improve with use.** Your brain cells are capable of making increasingly complex new connections throughout your life. And your neuronal endowment is so great that even if you lost one thousand brain cells every day for the rest of your life, it would still amount to less than 1 percent of your total. (Of course it's important not to lose the 1 percent that you actually use!)

The learning organization is comprised of individuals who know how to learn quickly and effectively. Instead of resisting change and new learning challenges, they embrace the unknown with enthusiasm and confidence. The first step in cultivating this enthusiasm and confidence is to realize that you were born with an amazing capacity for learning. Professor Pyotr Anokhin, a student of Pavlov at Moscow University, spent decades researching the number of possible thought patterns that the average human brain can make. He established that the minimum number of thought patterns your brain can make is the number 1 followed by more than six million miles of typewritten zeros. No one, not even da Vinci or Einstein, has ever come close to using his full brain power.

Why is it, then, that so many people seem to resist learning and change as they get older? In a nutshell, the answer is habit, unexamined habits of thinking and doing.

As we age, it becomes all too easy to get stuck in a routine. And often, our routine is accompanied by an assumption that education ends when we finish school, and that our mental and physical performance will inevitably decline.

> Iron rusts from disuse, water that does not flow becomes stagnant, thus it is with the human mind.
>
> —Leonardo da Vinci

At school most of us had little choice regarding the subjects we were supposed to learn. In art class you had to draw. In math class you had to do long division. In gym class you had to play dodge ball whether you liked it or not. Whether it was singing, drawing, shop, sports, or math class, almost everyone experienced the embarrassment of being pushed to perform publicly in an area in which they were unskilled. As adults, we can usually avoid the discomfort and embarrassment associated with learning something unfamiliar. We have more choice regarding what we do and what we learn. Most grown-ups choose to focus only on those areas in which they have obvious natural talent and avoid the subjects that were sources of discomfort in school. Schooling conditions many of us to avoid the new, the challenging, and the unfamiliar. As a result, many people become narrower in perspective as they get older.

Perhaps you've noticed that as you get older, time seems to go faster. So whatever it is that you've always wanted to learn, begin it now. You'll be good at it before you know it.

The most recent research into aging and human performance suggests that like Peter Drucker, Johann Wolfgang von Goethe, George Russell, Georgia O'Keeffe, Pablo Picasso, Mstislav Rostropovich, Martha Graham, George Foreman, Nolan Ryan, Giuseppe Verdi, George Burns, and Château Mouton Rothschild, you have the ability to improve with age.

A Sound Mind in a Sound Body

In a fascinating experiment, seniors were tested for mental acuity, after which they spent 15 minutes in an oxygen tent. The seniors' scores improved significantly when they were retested after the oxygen exposure. Researchers discovered similar improvements in mental functioning following surgery to clear the carotid arteries (the primary conduits of blood and, therefore, oxygen, to the brain). Your brain is a little more than 2 percent of your body weight but it uses more than 20 percent of your oxygen intake. Years of sedentary behavior and poor dietary habits can result in sluggish arterial blood flow to the brain, causing interference with memory and other mental functions. Keep your brain oxygenated and your mind sharp as you age by eating well and maintaining a fitness regimen that includes cardiovascular, flexibility, and strength training.

The key to this continuous improvement is to nurture a positive attitude toward aging as you maintain your fitness and challenge yourself with new learning activities. As a lifelong learner, you'll continue to improve throughout your career, making yourself increasingly marketable in a rapidly changing, competitive environment. The next time you are faced with a learning challenge at work or at home—whether it's implementing a new information or accounting system, integrating a new culture after a merger, or learning a new language or sport—you'll be ready to apply what you learn in the pages that follow to access and unleash that potential.

Overview: The 5 Keys to High Performance Learning

In addition to offering a simple definition of juggling, the title *More Balls Than Hands* also suggests the importance in a competitive environment of the ability to accomplish more with fewer resources. And accomplishing more with fewer resources requires a positive approach to learning and change. Individuals and organizations that embody high performance are characterized by their confidence and enthusiasm for new learning challenges. As you explore Part I of this book, which outlines the 5 Keys to High Performance Learning, you may begin to realize that your potential for learning and change is much greater than you might have imagined. Although each of the 5 Keys is useful by itself, together they add up to something greater than their apparent sum. They will help you unlock your potential for high performance as well as allow you to bring out the best in others at work and at home. The 5 Keys are:

1. Activate Your Brain's Success Mechanism

Your brain has evolved over millions of years to be the most powerful learning mechanism in all known creation. It is designed to help you survive and succeed in anything you do. Now you're about to learn the simple secret for activating and optimizing your brain's natural success mechanism. You'll probably find that this information is intuitively obvious, that it seems like something you already know. But you'll be guided to clarify, focus, and, most important, *apply* this understanding to dramatically accelerate your progress in learning anything.

Success

Webster defines "success" as the "accomplishment of what is desired or aimed at." In the pages that follow, you'll learn to clarify your desires and improve your aim. And you'll discover that success is best construed as what Coach John Wooden terms "the sense of satisfaction that you get from knowing you've done your best."

---

2. Transform Your Attitude Toward Mistakes and Failure

Imagine what you could achieve if you had no fear of failure. What would it be like if you could view your mistakes with affection? Have you ever considered that your ability to advance as a leader might be tied to your willingness to make mistakes at a higher level and that you can accelerate your progress in any discipline by learning to make mistakes on purpose? Revolutionizing your attitude toward mistakes and failure will liberate within you tremendous energy and enthusiasm for learning. You'll also discover how this **mistake-positive** attitude can help you create a learning organization at work. In the organizational world it's no longer enough to create an open environment where people feel free to acknowledge and learn from mistakes; it's now a question of how *quickly* your organization can learn.

3. Unleash Your Natural Genius Through the Power of Play

Creating a playful, open environment is a serious priority for organizations aiming to attract and retain the best people. On a personal level, you may find that for the first time since your early childhood, learning new things—even things for which you think you have little talent—can be engaging, enjoyable, and fun. This next key will allow you to discover that the process of learning can be as rewarding as the results you achieve. And you may be surprised to realize that as an enlightened adult learner you can learn faster than a child.

4. Achieve More with Less Effort by Cultivating Relaxed Concentration

When you watch a great performer like Tiger Woods, Yo-Yo Ma, Fred Astaire, Ella Fitzgerald, Kobe Bryant, Midori, or Meryl Streep, don't they make it look . . . *easy?*

Whether learning to lead, putt, or juggle, you will soon discover that the best results are achieved by using the right amount of effort in the right place at the right time. And this right amount is often less than we think we need. Most of us are used to getting results by trying harder, but with some things trying harder does not work. Greater effort can exacerbate faulty patterns of action. Doing the wrong thing with more intensity rarely improves the situation. Learning something new often requires us to unlearn something old. With this fourth key you'll discover how to undo old patterns of tension and stress, how to get more result with less effort. In the process you will discover the simple psychological and physiological secrets for achieving the state of "flow."

5. Develop Your Coaching Skills So You Can Bring Out the Best in People at Work and at Home

In 1973 I saw someone juggle and was immediately captivated by the beauty of this "moving sculpture." But when I asked this talented juggler to teach me, he said, "Take these three balls, throw them up, and don't let any of them drop!" Clearly, being a talented juggler doesn't make you a good juggling teacher. Starring on the football field doesn't guarantee that you'll be a successful football coach. Excelling in sales or design doesn't correlate necessarily with effectiveness as a manager of a sales or design group. Competence in coaching, managing, and facilitating is a separate skill set from technical competence in a given discipline. Of course, the very best coaches, managers, and teachers combine technical competence with an understanding of how to facilitate the learning process.

In the High Performance Learning program that forms the basis for this book, participants coach others in juggling before they've mastered it themselves. They are often surprised and delighted by their ability to help others progress well beyond their own level. The ability to help others perform at a high level is an important leadership skill. Often, the more you advance in an organization, the less likely you are to know about the specifics of the jobs of those who report to you. When you master this last key you'll know how to apply the learning process to bring out the best in others, whether or not you possess a specific technical competence.

Your First Juggulation

Perhaps you are beginning to get jazzed by the juggling metaphor, and while you're excited about applying the high performance keys in your life every day, you just can't wait to learn to juggle. If that's the case, please find three balls (tennis or racquet balls are good) and get started now by following these simple instructions.

1. Stand in a balanced, upright posture and enjoy a few deep full breaths, allowing generous exhalations. Start with one ball and toss it back and forth

from hand to hand in a gentle arc just above your head.

2. Next, take two balls, one in each hand. Toss the ball in your right hand; when it reaches its high point, toss the ball in your left hand in the same manner. Focus on smooth, easy throws, and **let both balls drop.**

3. Same as step 2, only this time catch the first toss. Let the second one drop.

4. Same as step 2, only this time catch them both.

5. Now you are ready to try three balls (you'll be truly juggling now because you'll have more balls than hands). Take two balls in one hand and one in the other. Toss the front ball in the hand that has two. When it reaches its high point, throw the single ball in your other hand. When it reaches its high point, throw the remaining ball. Do not try to catch them; just relax, and **let them all drop.**

6. Same as step 5, only this time catch the first toss.

7. Same as step 5, only this time catch the first two tosses. If you catch the first two balls and remember to throw the third, you will notice that there is only one ball remaining in the air. Catch the third ball. Guess what? You're juggling!

Of course, once you experience your first juggulation, you will probably wish to experience multiple juggulations. In Part II you'll be guided into the **juggling flow state,** where the balls seem to be juggling themselves. In the process you will learn how to improve the speed and quality of all your learning. Have a ball!

Part I

The 5 Keys to
High Performance Learning

Activating Your Brain's Success Mechanism: Comparing Vision with Reality

At Nike headquarters in Beaverton, Oregon, you can't escape the presence of Bill Bowerman. The main address "One Bowerman Drive" leads you to a place where Coach Bowerman's influence infuses every aspect of the company's culture. On their first day at work and every day thereafter, Nike's people are exhorted to "Remember the Man," and "the Man" is Bill Bowerman.

Nike's Jeff Johnson explains:

Bill Bowerman is the coach, mentor, and spiritual father of our company's founder, Phil Knight, and by extension of this company. More than any single person, Bill Bowerman personifies the spirit and the driving force of Nike. His attitude was, "if you have a body you are an athlete." He taught us that athletes, once inspired, perform beyond their previous imagined capacity.

Coach Bowerman reminds us that with courage, intelligence, consistent hard work, adrenaline, desire, and teamwork, we can get any job done. He inspires us to remember our mission: to make the best products at the greatest possible value and to get them on the greatest number of customers. In short, to swoosh the world. And he reminds us that in pursuit of that mission our jobs are to:

- coach, mentor and share our experiences
- have faith and confidence in our teammates
- work creatively, intelligently, cooperatively and consistently
- think outside the box, take chances, and risk being wrong
- forgive yourself and others for the mistakes you will inevitably make for they are all part of becoming better at what you do

Nike's vision/mission is clear and compelling. It's embodied in the image of one man who serves as the supreme corporate role model and is manifest in their instantly recognizable "swoosh" logo. Nike works very hard to measure performance—and fealty to the Bowerman creed—on a corporate, team, and individual basis.

By any standard, Nike is a remarkably successful company. Why? Because they do a better job than most of activating the brain's natural success mechanism.

Embracing your success mechanism is the first step in learning to "juggle." That is, it encourages you to have a positive attitude toward learning and change, which will greatly improve your ability to do more in less time or with fewer resources. The secret to success in learning anything is simple: Create a clear vision of what you want to do and then seek accurate feedback on what you are actually doing. Your brain has been designed, through millions of years of evolution, to move you toward the fulfillment of whatever it is you picture yourself doing. This success mechanism is hard-wired into your brain. You can take full advantage of it—as Nike does with Bill Bowerman's example—by seeking images of excellence in whatever it is you hope to learn or accomplish, internalizing them, and then relentlessly seeking accurate feedback on your performance.

You can activate your brain's natural success mechanism by:

- feeding your mind with models of excellence
- setting goals and clearly visualizing results based on your internalized model of excellence
- seeking accurate feedback on your performance

> Where there is genuine vision, people excel and learn, not because they are told to, but because they want to.
>
> —Peter Senge, *The Fifth Discipline: The Art & Practice of the Learning Organization*

⋮ Modeling Excellence ⋮

Any learning process or new activity you decide to pursue—in business, sports, or your personal life—begins with the formation of a picture in your mind's eye. If you want a promotion to a more senior position, you imagine yourself carrying out the responsibilities of the office to which you aspire. If you want to learn to ski, you're likely to begin with a vague picture in your mind of yourself gliding down a snowy slope. If you're planning to get married, you picture yourself and your partner living happily ever after.

Unique Human Advantage

Baby ducks learn to survive by imitating their mothers. Learning through imitation is fundamental to many species, including humans. As we become adults, we have a unique advantage: We can choose whom and what to imitate. We can also consciously choose new models to replace previously imitated but no longer functional models.

Since the learning process begins with the formation of a mental image, you might as well choose the best. If you want to become a leader, study the great leaders. If you want to become a great golfer, observe the best players. If you want to become a great juggler, spend as much time as you can watching great jugglers. Whatever your discipline, become a student of excellence in all things. Take every opportunity to observe people who manifest the qualities of mastery. These models of excellence will inspire and guide you toward the fulfillment of your highest potential.

The Wimbledon Effect

Each summer in England, the Wimbledon Lawn Tennis Championships are played over a two-week period. Tennis fans spend hours every day watching the matches on television. And tennis coaches around the country report a marked improvement in the performance of their students and club members in the weeks following the tournament. Now you can take conscious advantage of this **Wimbledon effect** in any area of endeavor by immersing yourself in images of excellence.

Bob, a hard-driving advertising sales manager for a major radio network, offered a sentiment that is not at all uncommon: "I've tried improving my golf game by watching great players like Tiger Woods, but it just makes me depressed. All I can think is 'I'll never be that good.'"

Well, Bob's probably right, he never will be as good as Tiger. But with a little coaching he can learn to use the example of Tiger and others to improve his game significantly. Instead of comparing yourself to or competing with your model of excellence, try using the following complementary strategies.

Let's say, for example, that you have the opportunity to spend a few hours watching a great golfer like Tiger Woods. How can you get the most out of your observation? Begin in the **open-receptive** mode, which I also call "looking through the eyes of a child" because children are so uncritical of everything they see. Enjoy a few deep breaths, allowing full, extended exhalations; "soften" your eyes—try not to focus on any one thing too closely—and take in the whole pattern of your great golfer's movement. As you watch, imagine your body moving in harmony with the golfer's rhythm.

When you're in this open-receptive mode of awareness, you avoid analyzing everything and can simply enjoy watching your model while imagining their ease and power spreading through your body. Immerse your mind and body in the images, sounds, and "feel" of excellence, and imagine them becoming part of you by psychological osmosis.

After activating the right hemisphere of your brain by uncritically enjoying your model of excellence, switch to the **focused-analytical** mode. In focused-analytical mode you'll activate your left cortex as you look for the specific elements of the great golfer's technique: note, for example, the positioning of the elbows and hands, body posture, facial expression, and breathing rhythm. As you study what the golfer *is* doing, you're also analyzing what he is *not* doing: raising his shoulders, holding his breath, etc. Observe and analyze the specific technical elements of the excellent performance, then make a detailed list of its fundamental strengths and weaknesses.

You should then switch back and forth between the two modes every ten minutes or so. After the time with your great golfer is over, imagine integrating and being able to apply everything you have observed into your own performance the next time you play.

Begin with a Clear Picture in Mind

In a recent High Performance Learning program at Nike head-quarters, I began the juggling lesson with a demonstration. First, I encouraged participants to observe me juggling in the uncritical open-receptive mode—"through the eyes of a child." Then, after just enjoying the rhythm, pattern, and colors of the juggling sequence, the group shifted to the focused-analytical mode, in which they watched me closely and analyzed my performance in a step-by-step approach. As one participant commented, "I was amazed at how much I was able to learn by just watching. Now I have a feeling for juggling and a real idea of how to do it. Of course, I know I'll have to practice a lot to make my vision real, but it helps tremendously to have a much clearer picture of what juggling actually is!"

Of course, even if a great golfer isn't available for you to observe in person, you can nurture your model of excellence by using video-tapes. Watch tapes of the greatest performers in your chosen areas of endeavor. Apply both modes of seeing on a regular basis, immersing yourself in inspiring images of excellence.

Catch Yourself Doing Something Right

In the old days, top collegiate and professional sports teams used to watch game films and point out all the players' errors. While this practice continues into the present, teams have added a new dimension. Now they watch the game films and catch players doing something right. Players are then encouraged to watch videos of their best performances repeatedly—

in order to imprint the image of high performance into their minds and bodies.

You can apply the same approach to modeling excellence in the workplace. Start by identifying the competencies that are most important for your development. Then seek out role models or mentors for each one. You can improve your listening skills, for example, by emulating the best listeners you know. You can do the same with presentation skills, creative thinking, or project management. You can complement your observation and work with role models by seeking out books and videos that highlight the best principles and practices in the areas you aim to develop.

Internalizing Your Model of Excellence

As you immerse yourself in images of excellence you will begin to internalize them, creating your own mental excellence video with yourself as the star. This means you can, for example, begin practicing your juggling without picking up a ball, or improve your presentation skills before approaching the podium. The ability to consciously create an internal vision is a capacity that everyone has, waiting to be used to its full potential. Your brain is the greatest audio/video producer on the planet, able to produce many more scenes than have been created in the history of Hollywood. High performers in all disciplines have always used this power of creative visualization to lead them in crafting and fulfilling their dreams.

A growing body of evidence from experiments performed by psychologists around the world shows that creative visualization improves performance. Australian psychologist Alan Richardson conducted one of the classic experiments:

Richardson took three groups of people and tested their performance in basketball free throw shooting. Then the first group was told to practice every day for twenty minutes. The second group was instructed to forget about basketball altogether. The third group was asked to sit down, relax, and imagine themselves successfully sinking free throws for twenty minutes. Richardson instructed them to feel themselves releasing the ball, see the perfect arc, hear the sounds of the ball swishing through the nets, and feel the satisfaction resulting from that imagined success.

At the end of the experimental period, he retested the three groups and found that the first group, the ones that actually practiced each day, had improved their shooting by 24 percent. The second group, who were instructed to completely forget about basketball, made no improvement. The third group, the ones who were told to "just think about it," improved their shooting by 23 percent!

Other experimenters have replicated Richardson's results, not only in basketball free throw shooting but also in a wide range of other activities including juggling, dart throwing, ring tossing, skating, and karate. The conclusion is that visualization, especially when it is multisensory, can produce a marked increase in actual performance.

⋰ The Mind-Body Connection ⋰

Visualization works because the mind and body are linked in a profoundly intimate way. When you imagine yourself tossing a ball to a point in space, for example, you are subtly activating the neuromuscular pathways that will perform the action. Science is deepening our understanding of this connection. One of the most fascinating studies was conducted by Dr. John Basmajian of Emory University. Basmajian took extremely fine electrodes and connected them to single motor muscular units in people's forearms. By connecting these electrodes to an oscilloscope and an audio amplifier, Basmajian was able to record the electrocontractile pattern of each motor unit. This unit consisted of one nerve cell and a tiny muscle bundle, and each one showed its own unique pattern, different from the others in both the shape of the spikes on the oscilloscope and in a corresponding popping sound recorded on the audio amplifier.

Basmajian then discovered that *just by envisioning it, people could change the firing pattern of each individual unit.* He reported that "most persons became so skilled they could produce a variety of rhythms such as doublets, triplets, galloping rhythms, and even complicated drum rolls and drum beats."

In other words, creative visualization affects individual motor units and energizes the muscle groups needed to perform an action. Sharpening the image of the perfect toss in your mind's eye makes it much more likely that the ball will land in your hand.

90 Percent of the Game Is Half Mental

Tiger Woods and Jack Nicklaus agree that at the top level of professional golf, 80 percent of success depends on the visualization of excellence in the golfer's mind; or, in the inimitable words of Yogi Berra, "Ninety percent of the game is half mental." Muhammad Ali's visualization was so powerful he "injected" his images of success into the minds of his opponents, encouraging them to fall when he said they would. Bodybuilding legend Arnold Schwarzenegger cultivated his power of visualization, developing vivid, specific imagery for each of his muscles. When working on his biceps, for example, he pictured them as mountains—the secret, he proclaimed, of his amazing 22-inch arms. Schwarzenegger then applied the same power of creative visualization to his successful career in the movies.

Like athletes, great artists also visualize their creations and then apply discipline to bring those images to life. Leonardo da Vinci emphasized the importance of creating a perfect image in the mind's eye before putting the brush to the canvas. Michelangelo reported seeing the image of his sculpture in the stone and then simply removing the unnecessary material until only his perfect vision remained. Picasso commented: "It would be very interesting to record photographically, not the stages of a painting, but its metamorphoses. One would see perhaps by what course a mind finds its way towards the crystallization of its dream. But what is really very serious is to see that the picture does not change basically, that the initial vision remains almost intact."

In many other areas, from business to medicine and beyond, success follows those who formulate internalized models of excellence and, by persistence and dedication, make them real. Stephen Covey, author of *The 7 Habits of Highly Effective People,* calls this "beginning with the end in mind." Covey emphasizes that all accomplishments are created twice: first in the mind and then in the world.

Most of us visualize on a daily basis, but we often do it unconsciously and negatively. It is called worrying. What happens to your body when you worry? You tense up. Muscle contraction and trouble breathing are part of a common pattern that can become a self-fulfilling prophecy of failure. Instead, learn to use positive, creative visualization to prepare yourself for success. As you practice positive visualization, the energy that fueled your worry will transform into enthusiasm for making your dreams come true.

Tips on Creative Visualization

To get the most from your visualization practice, bear in mind the following simple points:

• Anyone can visualize. If you feel you do not have the ability to visualize, ask yourself if you can describe—even roughly— the following objects: your car; a giraffe; your home; a lemon. Obviously, you can.

Some people see these images vividly while others find that their mind's eye does not offer up clear pictures. The benefits of visualization practice accrue even if you just think about your desired goal without seeing clear images in your mind's eye.

The ability to picture a desired outcome is built into your brain, and your brain is designed to help you succeed in matching that picture with your performance.

• Make your visualization multisensory. The more thoroughly you involve your senses, the more powerful your visualization becomes. As you visualize juggling, for example, imagine feeling the shape, texture, and weight of the balls in your hands. See the color of the balls and picture their perfect trajectory. Listen to the rhythmic sounds of a perfect cascade.

Unless you are already a master, your visualization will have gaps in it. Take advantage of whatever images you have, and over time use your models of excellence to furnish your visualization with greater sensory depth and richness.

• Practice. Just like any other skill, your ability to visualize will improve with repetition. Commit yourself to a regular schedule of mental practice. Some of the best times for practicing visualization include:

  • in the morning upon waking
  • at night just before you go to bed
  • when riding in a train, plane, boat, or auto
  • when taking a break from work
  • after exercise
  • or any time when your body is relaxed and your mind is free

• Visualize outside-in and inside-out. When visualizing, it's useful to imagine that you are watching yourself from the outside. For example, if you are visualizing an important presentation, watch yourself from the perspective of the audience. Then reenter your own body and visualize your perfect presentation from the inside out. Experiment with merging your inner and outer visualizations.

• Distinguish between fantasy and visualization. It's fun to fantasize about being a great presenter, leader, athlete, or juggler, but fantasizing is not the same as visualizing. A fantasy does not require conscious attention and it is not as focused or energizing as a visualization. Visualization is conscious work. Of course, your fantasies and daydreams may plant the seeds for your visualizations, but dreams become real only as the result of work that takes place first in the mind, then in the world.

• Become your vision. Become your model of excellence. Bring commitment and passion to your vision. Great actors report becoming one with the characters they play. Do the same with your models of excellence.

• Keep it positive and focus on the here and now. When doubts, fears, or negative images arise, acknowledge them, and then reinforce your image of success. See yourself succeeding *now.*

> Besides providing an opportunity to balance my body and mind in the midst of multiple pressing priorities, juggling reminds me to pause and picture the outcome I want before grasping after results. Whether I'm learning a new juggling pattern or managing my team, my success flows from the ability to see the results in my mind's eye first, and then to clearly visualize the process for achieving them.
>
> —Dennis McIntosh, vice president of SBLI Mutual Life Insurance

⋮ Embracing Reality ⋮

Models of excellence and creative visualization are necessary ingredients in achieving high performance, yet they are insufficient on their own. In order to progress in any discipline, you must be able to compare your visualization of excellence with your current level of performance.

You need accurate feedback—from colleagues, bosses, coaches, teachers, critics, and friends—to lead you effectively and efficiently to your goals. Create a clear picture for yourself of where you want to go, and make an honest assessment of where you are now. Your awareness of the gap between a goal you passionately want to reach and an accurate assessment of your present status creates tension. **The willingness to embrace this tension with a positive attitude is a distinguishing feature of the most effective learners.**

Sometimes, however, it can be difficult to receive an accurate assessment of your present status. If you've ever observed yourself on video in a training situation, you may have been surprised by what you saw. Whether rehearsing a major presentation or working on your backhand, it's often amazing, and more than a bit disconcerting, to discover the discrepancy between self-perception and the truth the video reveals.

We live inside ourselves, so it's difficult to view ourselves from the outside. When learning to juggle, for example, you may *think* that you are throwing the balls up in staggered timing (cascading), when in reality you are making the common error of handing them across the bottom (showering). You will remain unaware of your mistake until you see yourself in a mirror or video, or receive feedback from a partner or a coach.

Of course, discrepancies between self-concept and reality are common in more than just physical performance. They affect all aspects of life, from the bedroom to the boardroom. Sigmund Freud emphasized that "it is an undoubted fact that disagreeable impressions are easily forgotten." They are also easily ignored. Even when accurate information is available, fear will often prevent us from acknowledging it. Many of us grow up with the idea that mistakes are bad, linking our self-esteem with continued successes. So in order to validate our experience of success, we unconsciously avoid information that suggests otherwise.

In other words, we all have blind spots. And as we become more successful, the blind spots can become that much more insidious. When work performance and self-esteem are linked, our resistance to feedback can become entrenched and we can easily be seduced into "believing our own publicity." There's a fine line between being surrounded by a supportive team and allowing oneself to be shielded from challenging feedback by yes-men. Despite the growing prevalence of 360-degree performance review tools and comprehensive human resource competency assessment models, there is no substitute for the creative, ambitious person who actively wishes to change.

In order to optimize the brain's success mechanism we must relentlessly seek to illuminate our blind spots. High performance learners cultivate the confidence that allows them to be humble enough to accept information that doesn't fit with their preconceptions. They request, and carefully consider, feedback from colleagues and critics. Information that might once have been ignored or perceived as criticism is now accepted and welcomed as a gift for growth.

Perfect Practice

Does practice make perfect? Not necessarily. In the words of legendary football coach Vince Lombardi, "Practice doesn't make perfect. Perfect practice makes perfect." Coach Lombardi reminds us that practice based on an incomplete model and/or inaccurate feedback can lead to suboptimal performance.

The Accelerated Learning Spiral

Your full capacity for learning blossoms when you have the following ingredients: 1) a vivid visualization of success based on a model of excellence, and 2) accurate feedback on your performance. Both ingredients are essential. If you have a clear vision but inaccurate feedback, you will be deluded, living in a fantasy world. If you have accurate feedback but are without vision, you will be uninspired and stagnant. If you have neither, then you probably wouldn't be reading this book.

The gap between your vision of excellence and the objective data on your actual performance should energize your learning process. When you embrace this creative tension between where you are and where you want to be, you activate your brain's success mechanism, which results in a continuous, positive spiral that accelerates you toward the realization of your goals.

Your brain is an evolutionary success mechanism, and this comparison process is its operational secret. As you come to understand and practice it, your success in juggling, both in business and in life, will grow.

> The key is to learn from them [mistakes] as fast as possible, and make changes as soon as you can. That's not always easy to do because ego and pride get in the way, but you have to put all that aside and look at the big picture.
>
> —Tiger Woods on seeking accurate feedback

②

Learning to Love Your Mistakes: Succeeding by Speeding Up Your Failure Rate

---

"If you want to succeed, double your failure rate."

—Thomas Watson, founder of IBM

Trace the profit patterns of any Fortune 500 company for a few years and you'll observe significant ups, downs, and plateaus. But overall, the best companies show a consistent trend toward improvement and growth. Of course, a significant percentage of companies drop out of the 500 every year, and over a twenty-year period more than 30 percent go out of business altogether. What's the key difference between the organizations that disappear and those that continue? The ability to learn from their mistakes and failures and to adapt creatively to unpredictable circumstances.

The best organizations build environments that support risk taking and a creative approach to mistakes. The ability to learn from mistakes and be resilient in the face of adversity is the greatest long-term predictor of success for organizations and individuals. Great companies like Johnson & Johnson, 3M, and Southwest Airlines have developed corporate cultures that are **mistake-positive.** They encourage people to acknowledge, share, and learn from their mistakes quickly and effectively.

Johnson & Johnson, for example, is renowned for its innovative business practices and quality products. The tone for their success was set by the company's founder, General Johnson. In his classic *On*

Becoming a Leader, Warren Bennis shares the story of former CEO James Burke's surprising introduction to a mistake-positive culture. Burke had lost the company more than a million dollars through the failure of a new product developed by his group. Summoned to Johnson's office, Burke was certain that he was about to be fired. Instead, Johnson shook his hand and offered congratulations. Johnson told Burke, "All business is making decisions, and if you don't make decisions, you won't have any failures. The hardest job I have is getting people to make decisions. If you make that same decision wrong again, I'll fire you. But I hope you'll make a lot of others, and that you'll understand there are going to be more failures than successes."

According to Bennis, leadership can't flourish without a positive attitude toward learning and mistakes. To be truly successful, organizations must view mistakes as a normal part of the quest for excellence. Organizations that create healthy learning environments are those in which all individuals, *beginning at the top,* take responsibil-

> I believe in letting people know that if they make a mistake it's not the end of the world. What would be the end of the world is making a mistake and hiding it. If people aren't willing to make mistakes they're never going to make any right decisions. On the other hand, if they make mistakes all the time, they should go work for a competitor.
>
> —Sanford Weill, Citigroup chairman, quoted in *Reader's Digest*

ity for acknowledging and correcting their own mistakes. This **mistake-positive** orientation sets the stage for rapid learning, innovation, and superb juggling.

At 3M, for example, many of the most successful products, like Post-it Notes, Scotchgard, and masking tape, began life as apparent failures. As Professor Robert Sutton of the Stanford University Engineering School notes in his marvelous book *Weird Ideas That Work:*

> The sense that innovations include goofing up permeates 3M's culture. Its product developers haven't just been lucky. Nor are they necessarily more creative than their counterparts at other companies. Managers have simply been more receptive to the idea that a company can literally profit from its own mistakes.

Southwest Airlines is well known for its efficient service and excellent on-time record, and its employees pride themselves on having the industry's quickest turnaround time. They can land, unload all their passengers, clean, refuel, and be ready to go in an average of no more than twenty minutes. When a flight is delayed or a turnaround is executed below the company's high standard, they take, according to Richard Farson and Ralph Keyes, "a non-punitive, team approach looking not for culprits to punish but lessons to learn."

Unfortunately, the mistake-positive cultures of Johnson & Johnson, 3M, and Southwest are still unusual. In most organizations, fear of failure remains the dominant motivating force in everyday life. In a study of the decision dynamics of nine major pension funds, researchers discovered that investment decisions were not based primarily on ensuring the best possible return for the funds. Rather, they were consistently made in such a way as to minimize the accountability of individual investment managers. A major study of inefficiency and waste at the IRS concluded that the overwhelming cause of the problems was the unwillingness, at most levels of the organization, to acknowledge and correct mistakes.

The unwillingness to acknowledge and learn from mistakes is the source of many of our society's greatest problems. Watergate, the savings and loan debacle, President Clinton's affair with Monica Lewinsky, and the infamous Enron and WorldCom bankruptcies all were made dramatically worse by attempted cover-ups. Our growth as individuals and as a society requires us to transform our attitude toward mistakes.

⠿ Mistakes: A New Attitude ⠿

"They were as excited about failure as they were by success."
Tom Crouch, in *The Bishop's Boys: A Life of Wilbur and Orville Wright*

Everyone wants to be right, but what if our idea of right isn't right?

Many of us grow up thinking of mistakes as bad, viewing errors as evidence of our fundamental incapacity or worthlessness. But what if mistakes and failure are our greatest allies in making the most out of life? After all, you can't learn how to juggle without dropping the balls. You won't get your black belt in Aikido without learning how to fall. And, according to Nobel Prize winner Linus Pauling, you won't get a good idea without thinking of lots of bad ideas.

Intense global competition and accelerating change demand unrelenting innovation as expressed in the motto of Silicon Valley: "If it works, it's obsolete." Innovation is driven by experiment, and experiment yields many more failures than successes. Individuals and organizations must transform their attitudes to mistakes in order to achieve the speeding-up of their failure rate necessary to learn, innovate, and juggle in the face of change. What's required is nothing less than a fundamental redefinition of success, and of failure.

Rudyard Kipling proposed a redefinition of failure and success many years ago when he counseled that we "treat these two imposters just the same." But now we need a more radical redefinition. The evolving new paradigm requires us to do more to encourage creative mistake-making. As Professor Robert Sutton suggests in *Weird Ideas That Work:*

The excessive value that our culture places on success means that people who succeed may still get more kudos than they deserve from peers and outsiders, and those who fail may get more blame than they deserve.

To offset this bias, perhaps this weird idea should be: Reward failure even more than success, and punish inaction.

Of course, the purpose of shifting attitudes about mistakes and failure is to encourage the smarter communication and accelerated innovation that lead to high performance. One simple, practical way to help people make this shift is to begin learning to make mistakes on purpose.

Creative, Strategic Mistake Making

In counseling individuals and organizations to embrace mistakes and failure, it's important to distinguish between mistakes and failures made in the pursuit of excellence and innovation and those arising from laziness, incompetence, and ethical lapses. Clearly, we want to support the former and avoid the latter. Richard Farson and Ralph Keyes of the Western Behavioral Sciences Institute offer a number of criteria for distinguishing between excusable and inexcusable mistakes, adapted as follows:

- Was the mistake made haphazardly, or was it the result of a conscientious attempt to innovate?
- Was the mistake the result of ignoring feedback from those who might have helped prevent it?
- Could the failure have been prevented by basic due diligence?
- Was the mistake caused by a self-serving agenda rather than service to the vision/mission?

- Was the mistake exacerbated by ethical lapses or deception with respect to risk or costs, or was it truly an honest mistake?
- Was the mistake in question committed repeatedly?

"My winning routine emerged from a series of mistakes I had made in previous demonstrations."

—Tony Duncan, international juggling champion

Mistakes on Purpose

When you begin to learn to juggle I can guarantee that you'll drop the balls whether you plan to or not. But your efficiency and enjoyment of the learning process can be dramatically enhanced by dropping the balls on purpose. If you watch a skilled juggler, you'll notice the movement of the hands: a rhythmic, consistent pattern. What makes it possible for a skilled juggler to move his hands in the same way every time? "Practice" is the most common answer. Of course, this is true, but the real secret is *practicing throwing the balls to the same place every time.* If you throw the ball to the same place every time, it will land in the same place, consistently. This makes juggling easy. It therefore makes sense, in the early stages of learning to juggle, to focus primarily on the throw and not worry about the catch. You can accomplish this by dropping the balls on purpose.

By simplifying the task and focusing purely on the throw, you learn more from every drop. The result is that you learn to juggle faster and with greater pleasure, *and* you become a better juggler because you are practicing with more poise.

So when learning something new, anticipate mistakes and make them in a safe environment. For example, when learning to drive a standard shift car, most people become quite anxious when the car stalls, as it frequently will. This is particularly upsetting on a hill in heavy traffic. Instead, they should try the following:

Take the car to an empty parking lot and practice stalling on purpose. Discover what too much pressure on the gas pedal feels like. Explore the sensation of too little clutch. As you stall, relax. You will be calibrating your sensitivity and developing greater control. A brief period of practicing this **mistake on purpose** will result in a much safer and more enjoyable driving experience when you take to the road.

The road to excellence in the martial arts begins with an emphasis on learning how to fall and how to "lose." Martial artists know that if you are not comfortable falling, then your stance and balance will be weak. If you don't know how to be thrown, how to "lose," you'll never be able to properly execute a throw. Similarly, in high wire walking it is essential to begin by learning to relax when you fall. The relaxation allows you to develop the poise to stay up when you start to lose your balance. Of course, tightrope walkers practice with a safety net, martial artists use a mat, and new drivers should use a big, empty lot. Whether learning to fall or to stall, we learn best when we can practice making mistakes in a safe environment. Then, in the "real world," mistakes are less likely.

Promoting Cynicism and Low Performance

When potential clients call to discuss implementing a High Performance Learning program in their organizations, they are usually sincerely interested in creative change and innovation. But every now and then I get a call from someone who is just looking to put a Band-Aid on a problem by throwing some training at it. Talking about wanting to encourage risk taking without backing it up encourages cynicism and low performance. Employees react to discrepancies between a leader's words and actions like sharks responding to blood in the water. As Queen Elizabeth I commented, "How shall your subjects feel if your words are honeyed but your actions are envenomed?" To avoid promoting cynicism and low performance, leaders must be prepared to acknowledge their mistakes openly and in a timely fashion, and incentives and compensation must be used to reward the risk taking and mistake making that lead to innovation.

But how do you apply this process, so clearly applicable to physical activities like driving a car or martial arts, to improving your employees' performance? Senior executives and HR and training and development departments must take the lead in incorporating a mistake-positive approach to individual and organizational learning. Instead of "Training and Development," you might view yourself as "The Department for Constructive Mistake Making." Anticipate the possible mistakes in areas targeted for development and then create training that simulates what can go wrong. When people are free to fail in simulations, they are less likely to do so on the job. This mistake-positive approach to training goes hand in hand with an enlightened approach to succession planning. Every job should include a "mistake log" that is expanded and then handed on to each person who fills the position.

As Dr. Ruth Clark, president of Clark Training & Consulting and author of *Building Expertise,* notes:

In the middle of the twentieth century the training establishment in the U.S. was heavily influenced by behavioral psychology that discouraged the making of mistakes. There was concern that making a mistake would result in adverse consequences for learning. This approach to instruction leads us to a counterproductive attitude about the value of mistakes and errors during learning. More recent cognitive instructional views suggest an alternative perspective on mistakes. The cognitive approach advocates that some of our greatest learnings can come from making mistakes followed by reflection on what went wrong and why. It's not the mistake itself that is good or bad. It's what you do with the mistake. Giving learners opportunities to try out new skills and experience the consequences of errors in a safe environment helps build deeper mental models that will transfer back to the job.

This mistake-positive approach also applies to recruiting and hiring. Job interviews are much more valuable when the candidate focuses on sharing mistakes as well as successes. Debbie Benami-Rahm, corporate recruiter for First Data Corporation, understands this:

> In our interview process, we are, of course, interested in the successes and highlights of our applicants' careers thus far. Just as useful in the hiring process is obtaining behavioral examples from their past work experience that illustrate their biggest mistakes and what they've learned from them. If an applicant can't think of any mistakes or past work-related challenges, this can indicate that he's either too inexperienced or less than candid.

Failing Forward

Business legend Mary Kay Ash proclaimed that a mistake-positive approach was one of her secrets of success. She called it "failing forward." Soichiro Honda, founder of Honda Motors, also credits his phenomenal success to a mistake-positive attitude. He says, "To me, success can only be achieved through repeated failure and introspection."

Higher Level Mistakes

In juggling, after you've dropped the balls for the thousandth time, you may find that they start landing in your hands consistently. But perhaps you now wish to learn to juggle four balls. Or the famous "Behind-the-Back" trick. Guess what's going to start happening again? That's right! If you want to reach a higher level, the balls will have to drop again. After you've mastered four balls, you'll probably want to learn five. . . . Guess what? The balls will drop as you've never seen them drop before. Now that you are aware of your brain's success mechanism, you can begin to see your mistakes and failures in a new light: as an integral part of your continuous process of improvement.

The notion that people rise to a level of incompetence and then get stuck there is known as the Peter Principle. And it is often a function of intolerance for risk, and the unwillingness to make mistakes at a higher level. As you rise in an organization you must be willing to take higher levels of responsibility. The higher you climb, the steeper the potential fall. There are pressures when you are accountable for a budget of $50,000, but those pressures rise exponentially as the amount rises to $500,000, $5 million, $50 million, and so on. The potential for embarrassment is always there when you are speaking to a division conference, but it's much greater when you address the annual meeting or appear on live television.

Del Lewis has managed big budgets and appeared on television in high-pressure situations many times. His résumé reads as a series of great triumphs. After working his way through law school and serving in the Peace Corps, he worked at AT&T for more than a decade and was eventually promoted to president of C & P Telephone Company. A few years later he took over as CEO of National Public Radio, and then, in 1998, he was named U.S. ambassador to South Africa. Lewis attributes his success to his willingness to make mistakes at higher and more public levels. He chuckles as he shares his personal motto: "Success involves activating plan B." Lewis comments, "In the early days at AT&T the culture was all about sameness and minimizing risk. After divestiture, everything changed dramatically. Suddenly, creativity, openness to making mistakes, and the ability to learn quickly from those mistakes were at a premium. Many people weren't able to adjust. We invested a lot of energy aiming to change 'Bell-Shaped

Heads.'" Lewis adds, "It's funny, but when I'm introduced as a commencement speaker or as a new board member they always hit the highlights of my résumé. But a chronicle of my mistakes and how I've aimed to learn from them would probably provide a much better way of understanding the success that I have enjoyed. And, as I've gained experience, I've strengthened my ability to recover quickly from setbacks and to learn faster from mistakes."

Mitsugi Saotome is an 8th Dan Aikido master and a direct student of Morihei Ueshiba, known as O Sensei (Supreme Grandmaster), the legendary founder of Aikido. Saotome, who is renowned for his seemingly flawless, effortless mastery of this complex martial art, explains that as a student in Japan he was awed by the apparent perfection of his teacher. "Your technique is perfect!" Saotome once commented to his teacher. "You never make mistakes!" O Sensei replied, "Ah, Saotome, I make mistakes all the time. I just correct them so quickly that you can't see it."

"Fall down seven times, stand up eight."
—Japanese proverb

∴ Trial and Error: Confidence and Success ∴

"A man's errors are his portals of discovery."
—James Joyce

Ironically, our willingness to embrace mistakes and failure often depends on our level of confidence in our ability. Confidence in one's ability to learn from mistakes builds success, and success builds more confidence to make more mistakes. You can develop greater confidence in your learning ability by cultivating a practical appreciation of the capacity and design of your brain and then approaching learning challenges in a "brain-friendly" fashion.

Once you have chosen, observed, and internalized your models of excellence, you will unleash the vast learning power of your brain by embracing the process of trial and error. In the words of contemporary Renaissance man/genius Buckminster Fuller, "The human brain is a trial-and-error mechanism." Fuller emphasized that the word "error" describes a process designed to ensure progress.

Fuller's prescription for the realization of our vast learning potential was passionate experimentation and engagement, focusing equal attention on successes and failures. The path of High Performance Learning invites us to enjoy immersing ourselves in the learning *process,* as we come to view success and failure with equanimity.

So, any learning experience—mastering a new information technology, speaking a new language, or improving your skills in presentation, tennis, golf, or juggling—is best viewed as a journey toward your continually evolving goals. A typical pathway is shown on page 30.

Sometimes, despite our best efforts, we find ourselves stuck on a plateau or even getting worse at our chosen endeavor. These points in the learning process, which we all experience, can be dangerous. It's at these moments that frustration can lead to feelings of hopelessness, despair, and fear of fundamental inadequacy, causing many people to give up.

Classic expressions of frustration include "See, I told you I was no good," "I knew it was impossible," "I've never been very good at this sort of thing," "Perhaps I should try something else," "I stink," "I can't," "I'll never get this," and "Either you've got it or you don't, and I don't."

When you come to one of these stages, you must:

- seek accurate feedback on your performance
- acknowledge and accept your current reality

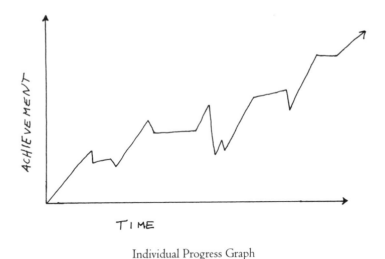

ACHIEVEMENT

TIME

Individual Progress Graph

- refine and then revivify your vision of excellence
- recognize that a drop in performance is not a sign of fundamental incapacity, but rather, *an integral part of your natural path to improvement*
- carry on

Of course, each individual's performance graph is unique, but all contain the fundamental elements of progress, failure, and plateaus.

The general pattern of your graph will be *toward the realization of your vision,* and your own individual progress toward that success will be unique, incorporating all the ups and downs of your own learning rhythm. The overall group graph, as an average of *all* the individual graphs, will be a smooth curve of average progress.

 "Fix Your Course to a Star"

It's easy to be a confident, mistake-positive thinker when everything is going your way. The real test comes in the face of extended

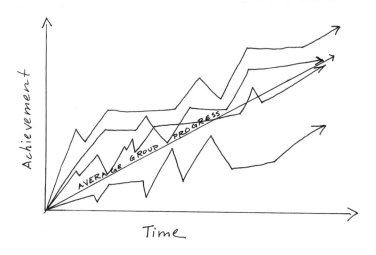

Group Progress Graph

plateaus and the steep drops in progress that are often labeled as "failure." According to psychologist Karen Horney, most of what people describe as failure in their lives is a function of withholding commitment. In other words, they give up prematurely and label the experience a failure. Horney observed that most people succeed when they *commit* to do whatever it is they want to do in life.

Commitment and persistence form the underpinnings of high performance and achievement in all areas of life. As you deepen your understanding of your brain's innate success mechanism, you'll naturally adopt the resilient, optimistic attitude that will lift you out of life's troughs. Dr. Martin Seligman, author of *Learned Optimism,* has demonstrated over more than three decades of research that optimists achieve dramatically better results in all areas of life simply because they don't give up in the face of adversity. And because your brain is designed to be the most powerful learning and problem-solving mechanism in the known universe, you will ultimately tend to succeed if you stay actively engaged in whatever problem you are attempting to solve.

As Walt Hriniak, batting coach for the Chicago White Sox, points out, the critical distinguishing characteristic of the best batters is their ability to deal with slumps. In his own words, "I don't care who you are, if you're one of the great stars of all time, making millions of dollars or some Little League kid, some day you're gonna stink." Hriniak emphasizes that all the best hitters, at one time or another, experience major batting slumps. He states that "the ability to maintain a good attitude when things aren't going your way" is the key to breaking out of a slump. Hriniak emphasizes that even the greatest hitters fail in 60 percent to 70 percent of their trips to the plate. Yet they approach every opportunity with a 100 percent commitment to success.

Creativity Is 99.7 Percent Failure

Japan has suffered from an economic malaise that has lasted more than ten years. In an effort to promote prosperity through innovation, challenges are being raised to the society's traditional view of mistakes and failure as causes for shame and mortification. A report in the Sunday, May 18, 2003, edition of *The New York Times* noted that "a growing number of scientists, businessmen and even politicians . . . are going public with their foibles." This effort is being led by the Japanese government-sponsored Failure Database Project. The database invites users to view its catalog of more than six hundred examples of Japanese faux pas in a constructive light. The *Times* adds that the database "will be used to help instructors plan motivational workshops on the beauty of failure." Echoing Edison, engineering Professor Yotaro Hatamura, who runs the Failure Database Project, comments: "Creativity is 99.7 percent failure."

This commitment in the face of adversity is a characteristic of genius in all walks of life. Thomas Edison failed many times in his attempt to perfect electric lighting. After his experiments blew up three laboratories, his friends urged him to try something else. Edison replied that as a result of his errors he now knew more than ever and that his success was inevitable. When Einstein's father asked Albert's schoolmaster what career path his son should follow, the teacher replied, "It does not matter, he will never make a success of anything." Gregor Mendel, pioneer of the modern science of genetics, flunked biology.

Winston Churchill, Charles Darwin, W. B. Yeats, Abraham Lincoln, Hans Christian Andersen, General George Patton, Gustave Flaubert, Marie Curie, Thomas Jefferson, and Leonardo da Vinci all paid tribute to the role of learning from mistakes as essential to their development. As Jefferson wrote, "Error is the stuff of which the web of life is woven: and he who lives longest and wisest is only able to weave out the more of it." And Leonardo, perhaps history's greatest genius, experienced many failures, including his flying machine that never got off the ground, his disastrous attempt to divert the course of the river Arno for the Florentine government, and his twenty-four-foot-high equestrian sculpture that was never completed. But his mistake-positive attitude was evident in his notes to himself: "All obstacles can be overcome through commitment," and "Fix your course to a star and you can navigate through any storm."

As you apply a mistake-positive attitude at work and at home, you'll liberate tremendous energy for learning and achieving. The energy you conserve by not worrying about mistakes can be invested in making problems easier to solve and life easier to juggle. By making mistakes on purpose, you'll take the fear out of new situations and nurture the positive cycle of confidence and success. As your confidence evolves, you'll embrace the opportunity to make mistakes at a higher level, thereby freeing yourself to achieve more than you might have previously imagined. Now that you know that you've got to drop the balls in order to learn, you'll be poised to respond to the bounce and ready for new tricks.

③

Unleashing the Power of Play: Seriously!

"Only those who are willing to risk looking foolish
can invent a breakthrough, give a speech, found a company,
or stand up for a principle."

—Richard Farson and Ralph Keyes, *Whoevever Makes the Most Mistakes Wins*

Marv Damsma is dressed in a flowing red cape and a blue body-suit as he struts the stage at an investment management conference. Billing himself as "Alpha-man," he draws waves of laughter as he captivates his very serious audience of corporate portfolio and pension managers with an unforgettable presentation on risk management. As director of trust investments for BP America, he and his team have successfully managed the pension fund more than fifteen years.

Damsma is a brilliant leader in a very challenging and serious business, but he emphasizes that "when you're investing billions of dollars of other people's money you are entrusted with a level of responsibility that is hard to overstate. But to do the job well you've got to keep perspective. Surviving the stock market's ups and downs can be very taxing, so humor and an open culture make it much easier to maintain perspective and create solutions to meet the fund's investment goals."

Damsma adds, "In our shop, we've always encouraged people to play with ideas. We've been brainstorming and juggling at our morning meetings for more than ten years. The result is an atmosphere where people feel free to express themselves and offer unique—i.e., 'off the wall'—ideas. While many ideas are reviewed, only a few make it through our rigorous analysis processes, but overall our team is much more productive in managing the assets."

Marv Damsma and other leaders of learning organizations understand intuitively the wisdom expressed by Plato, the father of Western philosophy, who wrote, "Life must be lived as play." The ancient Greeks knew that play was the secret of learning. As Roger Von Oech, author of *A Whack on the Side of the Head* points out, the Greek words for *play* ("paida") and *education* ("paideia") are slight variations on the same theme.

Play is the way animals and children learn. It is a powerful catalyst for the development of all mental and physical skills, including literal and metaphorical juggling, which makes it an essential ingredient in building and sustaining a creative, high-performance organizational culture.

In the words of renowned creativity researchers Robert and Michele Root-Bernstein, play is "a way of courting serendipity, the uncanny knack of finding valuable things not sought for."

And to relearn the art of play, it's best to start by modeling those who do it best.

> The sense of play is the essence of inventive activity. Invention begins in the joyful, free association of the mind.
>
> —Arthur Molella, director of the Smithsonian Institution's Center for the Study of Invention and Innovation

⚬⚬ Passion for Play ⚬⚬

If a baby toddles into a room full of adults, everyone turns and says something like "Ooohh, look at the baby!" The baby's passion, involvement, and alertness make it naturally charismatic.

Babies are passionate in pursuing their desires. They don't fear failure and they don't hedge their bets. As any parent will tell you, when a baby wants something—a toy, affection, a bottle—it goes all out to get it. As adults we are often too inhibited to play with babylike abandon. Our fear of failure can put a damper on our passion and full engagement. But what if the only real failure is the failure to play with all your heart?

True success means pursuing your goals and dreams with so much childlike passion that notions of failure and success become irrelevant.

Childlike passion is a hallmark of genius through the ages. As Sigmund Freud said about Leonardo da Vinci, "The great Leonardo continued to play as a child throughout his adult life, thus baffling his contemporaries."

A passion to play is the premium fuel for adult learning and achievement. In a classic study, chess masters were compared with chess Grandmasters. Researchers were unable to find any differences in IQ or memory ability between the two groups. The only factor that distinguished the Grandmasters was that they spent more time playing because they were more passionate about the game.

As George Bernard Shaw emphasized, "This is the true joy in life . . . being used for a purpose, recognized by yourself as a mighty one; . . . being thoroughly worn out before you are thrown on the scrap heap; . . . being a force of nature instead of a feverish little clod of ailments and grievances complaining that the world will not devote itself to making you happy."

Find healthy passion and nurture it. Be a force of nature. Play with all your heart.

Play the Greatest Game

> Learning is the greatest game in life and the most fun. All children are born believing this and will continue to believe this until we convince them that learning is very hard work and unpleasant. Some kids never really learn this lesson and go through life believing that learning is fun and the only game worth playing. We have a name for such people. We call them geniuses.
>
> —Dr. Glenn Doman, Institute for the Achievement of Human Potential

 Work as Play

Although they're invited to dress casually, participants often arrive at High Performance Learning seminars wearing business attire and serious expressions. They are usually stressed out from the intense pressures of their jobs and ambivalent about taking time away from work. As the program begins, I walk them through some practical exercises and engage them in conversation about their specific goals for the program.

Then I bring out the balls and we begin our first lesson in the art of juggling. Consistently, something remarkable happens: people start removing their jackets and loosening their collars; energy, smiles, and laughter begin to fill the room. Grown-up, serious managers become mischievous, animated youngsters as they rediscover the power of humanity's most effective learning mode: play.

Of course, for most adults, work and play are compartmentalized. But in the baby's world, they are integrated. A baby's "job" is to explore the universe, so for the baby, work equals play. A good example is the process of learning to walk. It involves a series of experimental attempts to stand upright and put one foot in front of the other. The baby spends hours crawling, nearly getting upright, falling, exploring, crawling, tottering, and falling, while laughing at both the successes and the failures. Can you imagine if after falling down a few times the baby said "Forget it! I quit! I obviously have no natural talent for walking!"

While learning to walk, the baby explores everything in his path: the taste and feel of the carpet, the tensile strength and smell of a piece of paper or Mommy's hair, the sound of a bottle banging against the crib wall. Like a little da Vinci, the baby delights in discovering all the aspects of his universe.

> # I play with microbes.
>
> —Response of Sir Alexander
> Fleming (discoverer of penicillin)
> whenever anyone asked
> what he did

Similarly, in learning to talk, babies play with sounds, words, rhythms, oral "feelings," volumes, pitches, and tones, constantly assessing the effects of the sounds on Mommy, Daddy, brother, sister, dog, or cat.

Young children display similar playing skills in learning almost anything. Engaging their natural power of creative visualization, they imagine themselves as different beings or objects. This creative imagination often leads children to remarkable insights, which are frequently unappreciated by the more prosaic adults around them.

For example, one day a friend of mine was sitting just behind a five-year-old girl and her mother on the subway. The train was accelerating and the little girl exclaimed to her mother, "Mom, wouldn't it be amazing if this train could keep going faster, until it was going so fast it could take us into tomorrow? We could then go home and tell Daddy what was going to happen in the future!" The mother, unversed in relativity theory, responded, "Don't ever say such a stupid thing again."

In this case, the little girl was playing with ideas in a way similar to Einstein's musings that led to the theory of relativity. Einstein imagined traveling out into the universe on an ever-accelerating sunbeam, and discovered tomorrow. Einstein attributed his special insights into the universe to his exploration of questions of time and space through the eyes of a child. As he noted, "A normal adult never stops to think about problems of space and time. These are things which most people think about when they are children. But my intellectual development was retarded, as a result . . . I began to wonder about space and time only when I had already grown up." Creativity researcher Howard Gardner refers to Einstein as "the Perennial Child," and attributes his genius to his ability to combine "the curiosity and sensibility

> Study and in general the
> pursuit of truth and beauty
> is a sphere of activity in
> which we are permitted to
> remain children all our lives.
>
> —Albert Einstein

of the young child with the methods and program of the mature adult."

A high performance learning culture demands that we integrate the "methods and programs of the mature adult" with the "curiosity and sensibility of the young child." In other words, play is an essential element in the culture of a learning organization. At Microsoft, for example, significant funds are allocated to activities that encourage the playful team spirit that results in high performance. Microsoft's Susan Greenberg notes:

> Fun is an integral part of our culture. In the twelve years I've worked here we've played whirley-ball, sung karaoke, learned to juggle, flown in hot-air balloons, taken sailing and rock-climbing lessons, visited museums and comedy clubs, and just generally maintained an atmosphere of play. It's not uncommon to attend an in-house party every couple of weeks, and when you walk through the corridors don't be surprised if you see people taking a break to juggle, play foosball or Ping-Pong. We work incredibly hard but the fun atmosphere persists, as a matter of fact, especially when we're under pressure.

Surely You Jest!

The word *juggler* comes from the Latin root "joculari," meaning *jester.* It's the same root for the words *jocular* and *joke.* Like many airlines, British Airways struggled for years with the problem of overbooking seats. They solved this problem, and a number of others, with the help of their internal "Corporate Jester." Paul Burch, a former marketing executive, wrote the job description and then took the position as BA's official "fool." He emphasized that the company's tendency to take itself too seriously was limiting its creativity and profits.

Trish Marosky, a district manager for Merck, nurtures an atmosphere of play by taking her staff to Chicago's famous Second City improvisational comedy shows and arranging for them to have lessons in improvisation. "We are invariably more productive, more creative, as a result of immersing ourselves in spontaneous humor," she says. The CEO of a multibillion-dollar financial services firm emphasizes that his clients always expect him to appear serious, especially when the market is down. But he confesses privately that the tremendous responsibility of his job demands the broader perspective that is nurtured by regular doses of humor and play. "Sometimes, when I'm presiding over an investment committee meeting and we're in the thick of very serious matters," he chuckles, "I conjure up the image of [Federal Reserve Chairman] Alan Greenspan unicycling on a tight rope while juggling five flaming balls."

The business best-seller *Fish* captures the spirit of the world-famous Pike Place fish market in Seattle. The authors explain that they were inspired to film and then write about this extraordinary workplace because people working there seemed so happy. And their happiness came from a feeling of work as play manifest in, among other things, their delight in juggling with the fresh catch of the day (don't try this in your own kitchen until you complete the advanced juggling chapter in Part II).

Uncorking Genius Through Play

Nobel Prize–winning physicist Richard Feynman describes his response to watching a colleague playfully toss a plate in the air: "As the plate went up in the air I saw it wobble. . . . I had nothing to do, so I started to figure out the motion of the rotating plate. . . . And before I knew it . . . I was 'playing'—working, really—with the same old problem that I loved so much. It was effortless. It was easy to play with these things. It was like uncorking a bottle. Everything flowed off effortlessly. . . . There was no importance to what I was doing, but ultimately there was. The diagrams and the whole business that I got the Nobel Prize for came from that piddling around with the wobbling plate."

⋰ Who Can Learn Faster, You or a Baby? ⋰

Like most adults, you'd probably answer the above question with: "Babies are better, faster learners." It is possible, however, for you, the adult learner, to learn even faster than a baby. You can learn faster than a baby if you are willing to combine a babylike playfulness with your adult cognitive skills and resources.

Take language learning, for example. Most people believe that a baby will learn languages far more rapidly than a 50-year-old adult. Actually, the fifty-year-old can learn languages faster than the baby, if that adult learns *as a baby does.*

Traditional language learning programs were based on an overly analytical approach. Students memorized verb conjugations and vocabulary words. It didn't work very well. Today the most effective language learning programs involve students in a total experience.

For example, in an Accelerated Learning Spanish class, students dress in sombreros and serapes. The walls are covered with colorful posters of Spain, Mexico, and other Spanish-speaking countries. Spanish music is playing in the background. The students are acting out a scene using only Spanish. When a mistake is made, the teacher simply repeats the correct word, phrase, or pronunciation, which the student then repeats. Emphasis is placed on expressive gesture and body language. The teacher regularly "catches her students doing something right." The room is filled with animation and laughter. This playful approach to learning isn't just more fun; it's much faster and more effective.

When meeting an accomplished juggler, people often ask: "Were you raised in a circus family? Were your parents professional jugglers?"

The assumption underlying this question is that one can acquire such a skill only during childhood. This assumption is almost right: One can master such a skill only by approaching it with the openness and enthusiasm of a child. It is the approach of a child that makes the learning possible.

What are the elements of the child's approach and how can you apply them to unleash your full learning power?

> The essence of creativity is not the possession of some special talent, it is much more the ability to play.
>
> —John Cleese

Curiosity: From birth, and some would argue even before, the baby's every sense is involved in exploring its world. The first years of life are characterized by a seemingly unquenchable thirst for knowledge. As soon as they can speak, children start asking questions: Why? Where? Who? When? What? How? The answers provide new data that form the basis for even more questions. An inquisitive child can take the most educated adult to the boundaries of knowledge with a few simple questions.

Curiosity—the desire to know, understand and explore—is the driving force of our natural learning mode of play. You can awaken and develop the power of play by asking questions and reaching beyond the answers with more questions. Leonardo da Vinci was, like most healthy children, insatiably curious. His curiosity was so strong that he wouldn't take "Yes" for an answer. When Nobel Prize winner Richard Feynman was a child, his parents nurtured his genius by asking him, "What questions did you ask at school today?"

Bring the unrelenting curiosity of the child and genius to your organization every day. Encourage off-the-wall questions and diverse perspectives. Passionate questioning is the catalyst of continuous improvement. When people in your organization are asking how to improve teamwork, customer service, quality, productivity, and cost-effectiveness with the same passion that a baby brings to its explorations, you'll be amazed at the high performance that results.

Openness and Wonder: Babies have an obvious advantage when it comes to viewing the world without preconception or prejudice. Their open awareness creates profound receptivity to new information. In a classic Zen parable, a master invites his student for tea. The master pours the tea. The student's cup is filled, but the master continues to pour. As the cup overflows, the student cries out, "Master, my cup is full, it's overflowing." The master replies, "So it is with your mind; if you are to receive my teaching you must first empty your cup."

You can "empty your cup" and bring more openess to meetings, for example, by playfully checking your preconceptions at the door. Try beginning creative problem-solving and strategy sessions by asking each participant to write down on a piece of paper as many of their preconceived beliefs and assumptions as they can. Then ask everyone to crumple up the paper and throw it out the door (actually, my clients seem to get a special kick out of throwing the paper at each other).

Seriousness/Intention: What is often dismissed as "child's play" is truly a very serious activity. Even though the baby often laughs while it learns, careful observation reveals that the child is dedicated, intent, and serious about the task at hand. Adults often comment that children have short attention spans; what that really means is that children do not necessarily attend to adult priorities. When engaged in pursuing their own agendas, children's power of attention is prodigious.

In many organizations people are afraid to be playful for fear of being dismissed as "not serious." They seem to believe that a tense, miserable demeanor gives the impression that hard work is being done. Instead, work smart. **Overseriousness is a warning sign for mediocrity and bureaucratic thinking**. People who are seriously committed to mastery and high performance are secure enough to lighten up. Create an environment where it is safe to be serious about the importance of play.

My friend Mara Kelley supports her burgeoning career as an opera singer with her day job in software sales. She told me about the presentation she recently gave to the very serious CEO and the anxious, distracted executive team of a major financial services company. A few minutes into her talk, she departed from the script and apologized to the team, in a playful tone, for interrupting their side conversations with her presentation. Then, looking the CEO right in the eye, she said, "You need a time-out. You seem much too grumpy to make such a critical decision—let's take a break for milk and cookies." Not only did she get the contract, but the CEO insisted that she be the exclusive representative for her company. Her lightheartedness communicated her unwillingness to be intimidated in the face of the overseriousness of her audience. As the marvelous pre-Socratic philosopher Heraclitus noted, "We are most nearly ourselves when we achieve the seriousness of the child at play."

Multisensory Awareness: Multisensory awareness, also known as synaesthesia, is a hallmark of genius. Albert Einstein, Nikola Tesla, Gustave Flaubert, Frank Lloyd Wright, Isadora Duncan, Richard Feynman, Henry Moore, Auguste Rodin, Leonardo da Vinci, and many other notables played with ideas by cross-referencing their senses. Nobel Prize winner Richard Feynman, for example, regularly tackled complex equations by assigning each element a color, shape, texture, and sound; when the colors, shapes, textures, and sounds all fit together, the equation, much to the amazement of his colleagues, was solved.

Children naturally use this multisensory capacity, sometimes equating color with sound, rhythm with shape, taste with touch, and sight with feeling. Because synaesthetic observations can seem bizarre

("Oh, Mommy, listen to that big red flower!"), these abilities tend to be restricted ("That's silly, flowers don't make any noise.")

You can improve your memory, creativity, and enjoyment of the learning process by cultivating this delightful ingredient of child's play. One of the most powerful ways to do this is to learn and practice **mind mapping.** Mind mapping is a nonlinear idea generation method developed by Tony Buzan that encourages you to express your ideas using color, imagery, and dimension in harmony with logic and analysis. Mind mapping will strengthen your multisensory awareness as you apply it to help you juggle ideas in planning and problem-solving.

> The words of the language as they are written or spoken do not seem to play any role in my mechanism of thought, which relies on more or less clear images of a visual and some of a muscular type.
>
> —Einstein on multisensory awareness

Repetition/Persistence: Babies are notorious for repeating things over and over and over again. Repetition gives the trial and error process time to work. Babies keep experimenting and exploring to find out what works and what does not. By repeating a new word or action for days on end, the baby reinforces new neural pathways. Like the baby, when you learn something new you begin to form fresh neuromuscular pathways. At first, these new pathways are tenuous, like the delicate tendrils of a seedling. Repeating a new behavior strengthens the new pathways and eventually roots the new learning in the ground of habit.

Many adults, however, try something once and, if they can't do it right away, assume that they just can't do it. Learning the intricacies of a new computer system, or understanding the adaptations necessary for doing business successfully in another country, isn't something that one can reasonably expect to learn overnight. But babylike persistence and repetition will make success much more likely.

Unconditional Self-Acceptance: Many of us agonize when we try to learn something new. We tend to internalize the views of our worst critics, berating ourselves ruthlessly for our mistakes. If we treated our children the way we treat ourselves, they would never learn to walk or talk. Can you imagine saying to a two-year-old, "If you can't pronounce it properly, then just shut up!" or "Stop falling down. Get up and walk straight or don't walk at all."

Scientists have begun to demonstrate that infants need love, in the form of cuddling and soothing encouragement, as a fundamental requirement for healthy brain development. Love is the greatest stimulus for the process of learning. If you watch a baby learning to walk or talk, chances are your heart will open and you will naturally offer your loving support.

When you were a child, your parents were responsible for nurturing your learning process with love. They did the best they could, given the limitations of their own upbringing. Now that you are an adult, you are responsible for nurturing your own learning process. Begin by giving yourself the love and encouragement you would give to a baby. Accept that your mistakes are merely stepping stones on your path to success. With self-acceptance as your point of departure, seek an accurate awareness of your current reality. Set ambitious goals and enjoy the tension between your goals and reality. Bridge the gap with joyful, serious play.

Achieving More with Less: Cultivating Relaxed Concentration

At every moment, everywhere in the universe, the least possible work is being done. Lightning strikes along the path of least resistance. . . . A drop of water falling in a vacuum is perfectly spherical, spreading itself out as little as possible. . . . The shapes of the continents, the size of a cloud, the design of our brains, the speed of the planets around the sun, the number of leaves on my sycamore tree and the exact order in which they fall in November: every feature of the universe represents the precise expression of this principle at work—or, rather, avoiding work.

—Dean Sluyter, *Why the Chicken Crossed the Road and Other Hidden Enlightenment Teachings*

When you are first learning to juggle, you'll notice that you have what seems like very little time between throws to catch the next falling ball. When balancing more balls than hands, each nanosecond seems precious. In Aikido, black-belt candidates have to pass a final exam—"juggling" four attackers simultaneously—and they usually feel overwhelmed by the lack of time available to respond to the onslaught. Just about anyone who works in today's business world knows this feeling. When you have 123 unanswered e-mails, 37 telephone messages, and 4 meetings to attend, it's easy to feel overwhelmed.

What if you could apply the same secret that professional jugglers, Aikido masters, and world-class athletes utilize to expand their perception of time, to get into the "zone," so you really could learn to get more done in less time? The secret is "relaxed concentration," applying the right amount of energy in the right place at the right time—also known as "appropriate effort" or "poise." It's not even something you need to learn; rather, it's more about unlearning.

This quality of poise is your birthright. Babies move without unnecessary tension, spines lengthening as they crawl, sit, or stand. Babies' relaxation in action gives them remarkable strength and resilience. As we unlearn unnecessary patterns of tension, poise reemerges, and with it a growing ability to learn with enthusiasm and joy.

 You've Got Rhythm

> *I think a band can really swing when it swings easy,*
> *when it just can play along like you are cutting butter.*
> —Count Basie

The natural quality of life is a rhythmic pattern of contraction and expansion, an essential pulsation that can be witnessed clearly in the simple amoeba. If the amoeba is poked or disturbed, it immediately contracts and its natural pulsation diminishes. Returned to ideal conditions, it resumes its natural rhythm. If the amoeba is continually disturbed, however, its healthy pulsation ceases.

This fundamental pattern is present in all members of the animal kingdom, including human beings. A healthy human baby manifests this essential pulsation. Breathing freely, its supple movements and unguarded expression project a radiance, a natural quality of relaxed concentration. This quality corresponds to a sense of wonder and fearless curiosity that allows the baby to learn at an incredible rate.

What happens to this freedom, openness, and passion for learning as the baby grows into adulthood?

It is compromised and often stifled by fear. Fear of failure, fear of the unknown, fear of ridicule, embarrassment, humiliation, rejection, and the loss of love. These fears affect us physically and psychologically, undermining our natural mind/body coordination and impeding our ability to learn. Reawakening your natural state of relaxed concentration requires transforming the energy of fear. Let's begin by understanding more about how fear manifests itself in the mind and body.

Most first graders display a fearless, natural curiosity and openness that are reflected in an effortless upright, alert posture. By second or third grade, however, you can see a decline in their poise. Kids start hunching their shoulders and tensing their faces as they become older, and by the time most students reach high school their bodies are both slumped and tense. This decline is partly a function of adjusting to a growing body while sitting in one place for a long time, day after day, year after year. But the greatest cause of the loss of natural poise is the insidious fear of failure or embarrassment.

Think back to first or second grade. Can you recall a time when the teacher asked a question and one of the children in your class waved a hand wildly—"Ooh, ooh, I know!"—and then blurted out an original, creative answer? But on that day the overworked, beleaguered teacher said, "No! Wrong! That's not the answer I was looking for!" And all the kids in the class started laughing. On that day a little voice in everyone's mind said: "Never, ever, ever, yell out a wrong answer again!"

Most of us learn that the game of school is not about self-expression, originality, or creativity. Rather, it's about getting the "right" answer, pleasing authority, and avoiding the humiliation and ostracism associated with mistakes and failing. The result is that we often develop a negative attitude toward activities or subjects that don't come easily. When the "right" answer isn't obvious, it becomes all too easy to shrug and say "I can't do this." This "I Can't" phenomenon creates a negative, self-fulfilling prophecy—mind and body conspiring to ensure failure. You can see a typical example of this vicious process in this story told by a seminar participant:

> It was choir day at school and all the kids were singing happily. Suddenly the teacher stopped the class and pointed out that someone was singing off key. We were told that every single one

of us would have to come up to the front of the classroom and sing a few bars solo so that the guilty child could be identified. When my turn came I was terrified. All I remember is feeling as if I was choking as I made a horrible screeching noise, and all the other kids started laughing. I've never sung since then. Every time I even think about singing I seize up.

Classic "I Can'ts" include I can't draw, work with computers, dance, do mathematics, get organized, be creative, speak publicly (according to the *Book of Lists,* public speaking is the number one fear, ranking higher than nuclear war or financial ruin). Others are I can't be happy, make enough money, get along with my spouse, and, believe it or not, I can't juggle.

"I Can'ts" are insidious because they are locked into the body as well as the mind. They sabotage your natural poise and the relaxed concentration that accompanies it. Rediscovering your natural state of relaxed concentration means liberating yourself from the psycho-physical effects of "I Can't" habits. The most insidious of these is called the **startle pattern.**

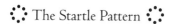 The Startle Pattern

What happens in your mind and body when you are afraid?

Dr. Frank Pierce Jones of Tufts University's Institute for Psychological Research performed an experiment in which he asked a thousand people to stand, one at a time, in their most comfortable erect posture. Jones wired each subject with electromyographical equipment, simultaneously setting up a series of stroboscopic cameras in order to measure people's reactions to an unexpected loud noise.

Jones found that every subject reacted to the sudden fear stimulus in an identical manner. The reaction involved

- blinking the eyes
- stiffening the neck muscles

- holding the breath
- contracting the major joints of the body

Jones called this reaction the "startle pattern" and in his subsequent research confirmed that it was a universal reaction to a fearful or negative stimulus. Jones noted that worry, general and vague apprehensions, anxiety, and depression manifested similarly, but in a slower, less dramatic manner. Jones observed that most people live every day in a modified version of the startle pattern. In other words, we tend to become psychophysically predisposed to react defensively.

A habitual startle pattern limits mental and physical flexibility and often results in counterproductive behavior such as avoiding new learning experiences and making excuses for failure even before trying. The startle pattern also explains the frequent gap between the words that leaders speak and the way in which those words are received and interpreted. If you talk about openness, innovation, and change but your body communicates a message of defensiveness, rigidity, and stasis, people will believe what your body communicates more than what you say.

The Emperor's New Clothes

In the more than twenty-five years I've spent working with organizations around the world, I've attended many meetings to launch a change. I've been present at the announcement of mergers, acquisitions, and restructurings, and witnessed the introduction of new visions, missions, strategies, and values, of new communications, training, hiring, and incentive programs. Many elements come into play in the effectiveness of these efforts, but the ones most likely to succeed are inevitably led by executives and teams free from "habitual startle."

How can you free yourself from the effects of habitual startle and unleash your natural poise, your capacity to learn and to lead?

Everything you've learned thus far in *More Balls Than Hands* is designed to help you awaken your full learning potential by turning "I Can'ts" into "I Cans." As you observe models of excellence, practice visualization, assess reality, learn to love your mistakes, and unleash the power of play, your confidence in your learning and leadership ability will grow. As your confidence builds, you will become a more successful juggler, both literally and figuratively, in your work and your life. Even better, your achievements will breed more self-confidence, launching you on a path to success you may never have imagined.

There's one more critical thing that has been implied throughout this book but now needs to be made explicit. To achieve excellence in learning and leadership, you must learn to access your capacity for relaxed concentration, to reattain your natural poise by freeing yourself from the legacy of startle. To begin, you want to prevent the neck muscle contractions associated with the startle pattern, which cause unreliable kinesthetic feedback and *the discoordination of the entire mind/body system.* As the home of your brain and the locus of your balance, vision, and hearing, the importance of your head balance can hardly be overstated. Moreover, receptors in your cervical spine (your neck) are responsible for a significant amount of the kinesthetic feedback that orients you in space. Your kinesthetic sense serves as a bridge between mind and body, linking your inner and outer worlds.

So, decontracting the neck muscles is the key to relaxed concentration. Easier said, however, than undone.

If the startle pattern is such a deeply ingrained habit, how can you unlearn it?

Give Up Trying Too Hard, but Never Give Up

In many areas of life it is possible to get results by trying harder, but with some things trying harder doesn't work. You will not, for example, improve your golf swing, your posture, your juggling, or your love life by trying harder. In these cases, greater effort can exacerbate faulty patterns of action. Doing the wrong thing with more intensity rarely improves the situation. Learning something new often requires us to unlearn something old. As Peter Drucker says, "Nothing is less productive than to make more efficient, that which should not be done in the first place."

⋰ The Alexander Technique ⋰

The most effective method for unlearning this pattern of contraction was developed by F. Matthias Alexander. Born in Tasmania in 1869, Alexander was a Shakespearean actor specializing in one-man shows of tragedy and comedy. His promising career was interrupted by a tendency to lose his voice in the middle of performances.

Alexander consulted the leading doctors, speech therapists, and drama coaches of his day, carefully following their advice. Nothing helped. The average person would have given up and tried another line of work. Instead, Alexander resolved to overcome his problem on his own, reasoning that something he was doing with and to himself was causing the problem. But how could he discover the specific cause?

Alexander realized that he must find a way to get objective feedback. He began to observe himself in specially constructed mirrors. After many months of detailed and thorough observation, he noticed a pattern. Whenever he attempted to recite, he:

- contracted his neck muscles, thereby pulling back his head
- depressed his larynx
- gasped for breath

Observing further, Alexander noted that this tension pattern (which Dr. Frank Pierce Jones would later call a modified form of the startle pattern) was associated with a tendency to:

- push out his chest
- arch his back
- contract all the major joints of his body

Alexander's continued observation confirmed that this pattern was present in varying degrees every time he spoke.

Noticing that this pattern of misuse began to manifest itself the moment he *thought* of reciting, Alexander realized that the key to unlearning it was to pause before reciting, thus preventing his habitual pattern of contraction. He would then mentally focus on the lengthening and expanding directions he wanted his body to follow instead—for example, "Let the neck be free, to allow the head to go forward and up, to let the back lengthen and widen." Alexander, creating an Australian version of a Zen koan, emphasized that these directions were to be projected "all together, one after the other."

Repeated practice of this new method produced dramatic results. Alexander not only regained full control of his voice, he also recovered from a number of persistent health problems and became famous on the stage for the quality of his voice, breathing, and general stage presence.

People began to flock to Alexander for lessons, among them a group of doctors who had an amateur theatrical company. The doctors began to send Alexander their patients with chronic problems, stress ailments, breathing problems, and back and neck pain. Alexander was able to assist these people in a surprising number of instances by helping them to learn a new coordination of mind and body.

The doctors were so impressed by Alexander's work that in 1904 they sponsored his trip to London to share his work with the international scientific community. He arrived in London and soon became known as the "protector of the London theater," giving lessons to leading actresses and actors of the day.

Alexander also influenced many notable figures in other fields including Professor Raymond Dart, Nobel Prize winners Sir Charles Sherrington and Nicholas Tinbergen, Sir Aldous Huxley, and "the Father of Progressive Education," John Dewey. Dewey wrote the introductions to three of Alexander's four books, proclaiming in one of these that Alexander gave him the means to translate his own ideals of progressive education into practical reality. In Dewey's words, "The Alexander Technique bears the same relation to education as education does to life itself."

Before Alexander died in 1955 he trained a number of individuals to continue his work. For many years the technique has been taught at the Royal Academy of Dramatic Arts, the Royal Academy of Music, the Juilliard School, and other top academies for musicians, actors, and dancers. The technique is a "trade secret" of performing artists including luminaries such as Paul Newman, Mary Steenburgen, Sting, Helena Bonham Carter, Paul McCartney, and John Cleese.

Alexander's work is based on a keen level of self-observation that includes:

- Developing an increasing awareness of inappropriate effort in such everyday activities as sitting, bending, lifting, walking, driving, eating, talking, and juggling. (Are you stiffening your neck and pulling your head back when you type on your keyboard, pick up your toothbrush, talk on the telephone, turn your steering wheel, or toss your juggling balls?)
- Attention to the natural flow of breathing, noticing and then preventing any interruption of this natural flow. (Are you holding your breath when walking up to the podium to speak? When picking up a pen to write? When meeting someone new? Or while catching or throwing a ball?)
- Maintaining "soft eyes": an easy visual alertness, a comfortable integration of central and peripheral focus. (Do you fur-

row your brow, squint your eyes, and clench your jaw when attempting to concentrate? Do you find it challenging to make easy eye contact with everyone in your audience? Does your focus get hard and narrow or diffuse and "spacey" as the balls approach their apex?)

> The means for keeping
> your eye on the ball
> applied to life!
>
> —Gertrude Stein's brother, Leo,
> describing the Alexander
> Technique

Alexander's work can provide the missing link in the discovery of relaxed concentration and the reversal of "I Can'ts" such as the notorious:

"I Can't Juggle; I Can't Even Catch!" Over the years I've worked with many students who complained that not only were they unable to juggle, but they weren't even able to catch a ball. When asked to give a demonstration of their inability, a common pattern can be observed: As the student grabs the ball, she tenses her neck muscles and holds her breath, and as she releases the ball into the air, her whole body contracts and stiffens, and in many cases she closes her eyes. As the ball drops, she cries "See? I told you I couldn't catch!"

When this happens I'll use a mirror, video, or mimicry to show the student what she is doing to herself (going into the startle pattern at the very thought of juggling). Then, as she learns Alexander's principles, she'll begin to be able to prevent this fear-based reaction by breaking the task into its simplest components (just throw the ball to the top of the box without even thinking about catching it; focus instead on letting the neck be free, head forward and up, back longer and wider). With a little patience and continuing attention to Alexander's directions for integrating her mind and body, the balls start to land in her hands. It's truly inspiring. Ecstatic students usually say "It's a miracle, it's the first time I ever caught a ball!" and "I was throwing two balls and all of a sudden the rhythm just happened!" After juggling three balls for the first time, a sixty-year-old student exulted, "I've just done the impossible!"

The Art of Doing Nothing

In 1975, I enrolled in a three-year teacher-training program in the Alexander Technique. For the first three months of the training I did no juggling whatsoever and focused instead on cultivating general poise and releasing long-held habits. This improved my mind-body coordination so much that upon my return to juggling I experienced immediate and dramatic breakthroughs. Tricks that had previously seemed impossible became easy, and I achieved my first five-ball juggulation. As Lao-tzu, master of Taoist wisdom, wrote: "The way abides in nonaction yet nothing is left undone."

The best way to learn the Alexander Technique is to have private lessons with a qualified teacher. Alexander teachers are trained to use their hands in an extraordinarily subtle and delicate way to guide you to free your neck and rediscover your natural alignment, in stillness and in motion. In the meantime, you can try the following simple exercise to promote relaxed concentration and free yourself from startle:

∴ The Balanced Resting State ∴

All you need to benefit from this procedure is a relatively quiet place, some carpeted floor space, a few paperback books, and fifteen to twenty minutes.

Begin by placing the books on the floor. Stand approximately your body's length away from the books with your feet shoulder-width apart. Let your hands rest gently at your sides. Facing away from the books, look straight ahead with a soft, alert focus. Pause for a few moments.

Think of allowing your neck to be free so that your head can go forward and up and your whole torso can lengthen and widen. Breathing freely, become aware of the contact of your feet on the floor and notice the distance from your feet to the top of your head. Keep your eyes open and alive, and listen to the sounds around you.

Moving lightly and easily, sit on the floor. Supporting yourself with your hands behind you, place your feet on the floor in front of you with your knees bent. Continue breathing easily.

Let your head drop forward a bit to ensure that you are not tightening your neck muscles and pulling your head back. Then gently roll your spine along the floor until your head rests on the books. The books should be positioned so that they support your head at the place where your neck ends and your head begins. If your head is not well positioned, reach back with one hand and support your head while using the other hand to place the books in the proper position. Add or take books away until you find a height that encourages a gentle lengthening of your neck muscles. Your feet remain flat on the floor, with your knees pointing up to the ceiling and your hands resting on the floor or loosely folded on your chest. Allow the weight of your body to be fully supported by the floor.

Rest in this position for fifteen to twenty minutes. As you rest, gravity will be lengthening your spine and realigning your torso. Keep your eyes open to avoid dozing off. Bring your attention to the flow of

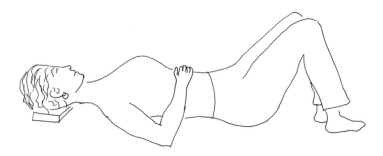

The Balanced Resting State

your breathing and to the gentle pulsation of your whole body. Be aware of the ground supporting your back, allowing your shoulders to rest as your back widens. Let your neck be free as your whole body lengthens and expands.

After you have rested for fifteen to twenty minutes, get up slowly, being careful to avoid stiffening or shortening your body as you return to a standing position. In order to achieve a smooth transition, decide when you are going to move and then gently roll over onto your front, maintaining your new sense of integration and expansion. Ease your way into a crawling position, and then up onto one knee. With your head leading the movement upward, stand up.

Pause for a few moments. Listen . . . eyes open. Again, feel your feet on the floor, and notice that distance between your feet and the top of your head. You may be surprised to discover that the distance has expanded. As you move into the activities of your day, think about not doing anything that interferes with this expansion, ease, and overall uplift.

For best results, practice the balanced resting state twice a day. You can do it when you wake up in the morning, when you come home from work, and before retiring at night. The procedure is especially valuable when you feel overworked or stressed. Regular practice will help you develop an upright, easy poise that encourages relaxed concentration in everything you do.

Our world is so wacky and the stresses so great that when it comes to nurturing relaxed concentration we all need all the help we can get. In addition to Alexander's work there are a number of other disciplines designed to cultivate relaxed concentration, including Aikido; yoga; the Feldenkrais method; Pilates; mindfulness meditation; Tim Gallwey's approach to "inner" tennis, golf, and skiing; and tai chi chuan. Each of these disciplines is worthy of further study.

The martial art of Aikido is particularly valuable for those who seek to master relaxed concentration. Aikido, literally translated as "the way of harmonious energy," is a Japanese martial art developed by Alexander's contemporary, Morihei Ueshiba (1883–1969). Ueshiba achieved an enlightenment in which he realized his oneness with the universe. He said, "The laws which define the structure and dynamics of the universe must become part of our awareness, for these are the same laws which determine the structure and dynamics of the body. The spirit that moves an atom, waves the sea, lifts the flames of a fire is also circulating in each human being."

Aikido is based on moving and breathing in harmony with this essential spirit, known as *ki, chi, prana,* or "the force." Ueshiba's insights of universal unity parallel those of spiritual masters from many traditions, but his particular genius was to develop a series of practical movements and partner exercises that, with regular and sincere practice, allow individuals to *embody* this perennial philosophy. One actually learns to be grounded but flexible like a willow tree, fluid like a wave, free like the wind, when facing would-be attackers and the stresses of everyday life. Indeed, there is no better way to test one's freedom from the startle pattern than to stand facing an attacker or attackers who are preparing to hit you on the head with a big stick.

Of course, learning Aikido takes many years of devoted practice. In the meantime, take a few moments once or twice a day to bring your awareness to the flow of your breathing. Breathe in through your nose and follow the breath all the way down to your center of gravity (the point just below your navel, known as *hara* in Japanese martial practice, *lower tan tien* in Chinese energy disciplines, and "guts" in the West). Using either hand, pat your lower belly a few times to help focus your awareness on your center. As the breath fills your center, visualize the inflow of positive life energy. Then, as you exhale, let go of stress, worries, and unnecessary tensions. After a few conscious breath cycles, imagine allowing your mind to rest at your center like a lotus blossom floating on a clear pond.

As you approach your meetings, e-mails, and phone messages, you can use this awareness of a still center within to enhance your capacity for relaxation in action. With a free neck, lengthening spine, and still center, you will be poised to act with greater efficiency and effectiveness in all your activities.

Of course, juggling itself is a tremendous tool for cultivating relaxed concentration. By practicing juggling you'll discover how to divide your attention appropriately between different pressing elements while simultaneously maintaining an awareness of the whole picture. Moreover, as you'll notice immediately, it's hard to think about anything else while you are juggling. Juggling practice will focus and calm your mind as it enlivens and balances your body. The rhythmic ambidextrous movement feels good and helps coordinate the two sides of your brain and body.

More from Less

You can cultivate relaxed concentration by making short juggling breaks a part of your work day. A good regimen is sixty to ninety minutes of work followed by five to fifteen minutes of juggling. As Dr. Tom Jenkins, formerly of DuPont and now with Dean Vaughan Learning Systems, comments, "We started making breaks for juggling a regular part of our meeting agenda. It lightens up the often heavy proceedings and we actually wind up getting much more done in less time." International business consultant and best-selling author Tony Buzan adds: "My clients in the IT department of a global investment bank sometimes work around the clock. In the midnight hours, they take regular juggling breaks. They say it keeps them more alert, less stressed, and better able to balance their intense workload."

After a while you'll probably find that you can maintain your poise, applying appropriate effort and relaxed focus, with one or two balls, but what happens when you try three, four, or five? How about flaming clubs, machetes, or chain saws? Maybe you are comfortable managing a group of ten people, but what about a group of a hundred, a thousand, or ten thousand?

As we attempt activities with greater complexity in business and in life, the challenge to our poise grows accordingly. We discover the increasing value of knowing what *not* to do, how to separate the truly important from the merely urgent and leave out the unnecessary.

"Geniuses sometimes work best when they work least."
—Leonardo da Vinci

⑤

Coaching and Coordination:
The Manager as Learning Guide

─────────

Nina Lesavoy has the Midas touch. As former head of sales and marketing at Chancellor Capital and senior adviser to the CEO of Invesco, and now as an independent consultant, she's brought in billions of dollars in investments for the funds she represents. In the process she's helped to make millionaires of many of her employees and associates. Lesavoy is low-key but sets high standards, and she has a special gift for bringing out the best in others. In other words, she's a great coach. She says, "Early in my career I realized that a collaborative team approach would generate the best results in the long term." Although she agrees that the investment business is highly competitive, she notes, "The rate of change is such that you may find yourself merged with a competitor and all of a sudden you're on the same team."

Lesavoy learned to juggle when Chancellor was acquired by LGT and she was sent on a three-week residential training program designed to integrate the diverse cultures of this multinational concern. Lesavoy admits, "I'm not gifted when it comes to the physical skill of juggling—although some improvement is evident—but I was delighted to discover that when we divided into teams it was easy to help others define and achieve their juggling goals."

The best managers, coaches, and teachers are skilled at helping others define and achieve their goals. Nina Lesavoy is able to do this in the investment business, where she is masterful, and in the art of juggling, where she's a novice, because she has an intuitive understanding of how to bring out the best in others. In this chapter we'll explore how to cultivate this understanding as we consider how the most effective managers and leaders apply coaching to facilitate high performance.

What's the difference between a coach, a teacher, a manager, and a leader?

Coach: Understands and guides the learning process. Acts as a catalyst/facilitator, making accomplishment easier.

Teacher: Gives instruction or imparts knowledge.

Manager: Monitors, measures, and controls the process of achieving goals. (To paraphrase *Webster:* one who contrives to make the budget suffice.)

Leader: Sets the vision and inspires its realization.

What do the best teachers, managers, and leaders all have in common?

They are great coaches.

In my High Performance Learning seminar, participants begin by observing and then visualizing the three-ball juggling pattern. Then the task is simplified: Everyone plays with one ball for a minute or two, followed by a demonstration of the two-ball pattern. Participants pause and visualize the two-ball pattern and then they divide into pairs: a juggler and a retriever/coach. The juggler tosses the two balls in the air in staggered timing and allows them to drop; the retriever/

coach picks them up and places them back in the juggler's hands. This team approach allows the juggler to focus on monitoring his own poise and the accuracy of his throws without worrying about mistakes. After a few minutes, the roles are reversed. When the class is ready to try three balls, the same process is applied—demonstration, visualization, practice—only now the class divides into groups of three, with one juggler and two retriever/coaches. After everyone has a turn, the groups debrief, discussing the implications of the juggling experience for accelerating learning and promoting teamwork on the job.

The best teams I've seen in twenty-five years of organizational consulting and coaching are characterized by a free, informal flow of information and a shared willingness to support, and seek support from, teammates. Dropping and retrieving balls together is a catalyst for enhancing informal connection and it encourages people to allow themselves to be supported. Yet despite the instruction to allow teammates to retrieve the balls, some participants rush to pick up their own drops. They find it very difficult to let anyone help them. It's not unusual for these same folks to have trouble delegating in the workplace. Moreover, the inability to allow others to help is usually a sign of a strong mistake-negative orientation, easily observed when someone grasps at each ball instead of focusing on the toss and letting the balls drop. (Of course, some people have the opposite problem: They focus *too much* on the process and never feel ready to attempt the catch.) Debriefing the juggling experience provides an indirect and nonjudgmental way to facilitate insight into these very serious issues.

One surprising insight that arises in almost every High Performance Learning seminar is that people learn better in a collaborative environment. Many of us were raised learning our skills in a competitive environment, and the notion of "grading on a curve" often forms the underpinnings of our learning paradigm. But as Richard Farson and Ralph Keyes emphasize, "The idea that competition leads to achievement is so basic to our way of life that the possibility of shifting to a more cooperative approach seems remote. In organizations of the future, however, this shift will be essential."

Teamwork, Heaven, and the Alternative

Former UCLA basketball coach John Wooden emphasized that "it's amazing what can be accomplished when nobody cares who gets the credit." But getting credit is often the thing people care about most. Peter Drucker, Russell Ackoff, and many other astute commentators on organizational life have observed that internal competition is often more brutal than external competition.

Over the years I've worked in many organizations filled with well-educated, intelligent people. Although pressures abound, most of these organizations are, by any objective measurement, remarkably affluent. Yet some are miserable ratholes pervaded by fear while others are fun, inspiring places to be. What's the difference? It is best summed up in the parable of the banquet table:

Heaven and hell are the same. In each place, people sit at large rectangular banquet tables. The tables are set beautifully and replete with every imaginable delicacy. All the diners in both settings have large wooden paddles strapped to their hands, and the paddles can't be removed. In hell everyone tries to feed himself, food flies in all directions, and fights break out constantly. In heaven everyone feeds the person across the table.

The simple practice of retrieving a partner's dropped juggling ball provides a lighthearted but memorable way to emphasize the heavenly virtues of teamwork.

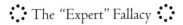 The "Expert" Fallacy

In his business best-sellers *Built to Last* and *Good to Great,* management researcher Jim Collins offers a cogent analysis of the distinguishing characteristics of the very best companies. Collins emphasizes that although many companies are born from the extraordinary vision and talents of charismatic leaders (a model he refers to as "the genius with a thousand helpers"), the truly great companies—the ones "built to last"—are distinguished by leadership that develops and capitalizes on the talents of lots of great people. In other words, the best companies create a learning environment and their leaders serve as facilitators. A facilitator is someone who makes learning easier.

Unfortunately, many managers make learning harder. A few years ago a rapidly growing trade-show exhibition company decided to explore a major upgrade of their information system. They spent a large sum researching the best providers and decided to invest in a state-of-the-art program. However, they made the mistake of putting their CFO in charge of the implementation and education process. The CFO was a quantitative/technological whiz who understood the intricacies of the new system, but he had no empathy at all for those who didn't share his gift, which, unfortunately, included almost all of the employees. He offered a series of implementation seminars throughout the organization but basically gave people the equivalent of "take these three balls and don't let any of them drop." People were afraid to ask questions because they didn't want to seem unintelligent. The result was disastrous; millions were wasted and most of the new system's capabilities remained dormant.

Like the juggler who instructed me "Throw these three balls in the air and don't let any of them drop," many experts aren't very good managers, coaches, or facilitators. Yet for some reason we often expect them to be, even though **there is no intrinsic correlation between technical competence and managing, coaching, or teaching skill.**

Experts are often poor managers, teachers, and coaches because they have forgotten how to put themselves into the mind of a beginner. Frank Lloyd Wright once suggested that an expert is someone who has stopped thinking.

Of course, the ideal manager or coach is one who combines expertise in a discipline with a practical understanding of the learning process. Even so, if you apply the following principles you may be surprised to discover that you can effectively coach anyone in just about anything.

It's what you learn after you know it all that counts.
—Coach John Wooden

> If your mind is empty, it is always ready for anything: it is open to everything. In the beginner's mind there are many possibilities; in the expert's mind there are few.
>
> —Suzuki Roshi, Zen Master

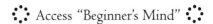 Access "Beginner's Mind"

Avoid the pitfalls of the "expert syndrome" by placing yourself in unfamiliar, challenging situations where you become "as a child." Beginning a new activity, allowing yourself to experience the awkwardness of not knowing, is a wonderful way to cultivate your "beginner's mind." As you struggle to remember the foot placement after your first ballroom dancing lesson, or the difference between masculine and feminine nouns after your first class in a new language, you'll deepen your empathy and appreciation for the person at work who is attempting to improve his presentation skills or implement a new accounting system.

⋮ Coach Unfamiliar Disciplines ⋮

> **In the master's secret mirror,
> even at the moment of
> highest renown and
> accomplishment, there is an
> image of the newest student
> in class, eager for
> knowledge, willing to play
> the fool.**
>
> —George Leonard, *Mastery*

One of the great ways to grow as a facilitator is to challenge yourself to help others learn subjects which you have not mastered yourself. This is an essential skill for all managers, and it becomes more important as you rise to more senior positions. Apply your powers of observation and knowledge of the learning process to facilitate learning in unfamiliar disciplines.

Golf Tips from a Nongolfer

On a free afternoon in the midst of a five-day residential High Performance Learning program, Dave asked me for help with his golf game. Despite never having played golf before, I agreed. Dave explained that he had a hitch in his swing that he couldn't seem to eliminate. I watched him swing a few times, and noticed that he was tensing his right shoulder at the beginning of every backswing. I asked him to bring his awareness to his shoulder on the next few swings, but he said that he didn't notice anything unusual. I realized that telling

Dave about the likely cause of his hitch without guiding him to discover it himself would probably only make things worse. Dave needed clearer feedback, so I gently put my hand on his shoulder and asked him to try the swing again. Dave exulted, "I'm raising my shoulder! That's the cause of this darn hitch." On his next shot Dave hit a perfect drive that hit the pin, and I retired from coaching golf.

Facilitate Relaxed Concentration

Poise is often the missing link in a learning situation. Guide your people to discover and release unnecessary tensions, as I did with Dave. Remember that most people do not know how to translate the command *"Relax!"* into physical reality. So instead, create an atmosphere that is conducive to relaxed concentration.

Never Use Humor

Just kidding! Humor is one of the most elegant ways to facilitate an atmosphere of relaxed concentration. Dispel anxiety, stress, and fear with laughter.

Expect Success and Demand Excellence

> It's a funny thing about life;
> if you refuse to accept
> anything but the very best,
> you very often get it.
>
> —Somerset Maugham

Challenge your team to move beyond self-imposed boundaries to new levels of excellence. Expecting your people to excel demonstrates your confidence in their ability, and it gets results. A growing body of research shows that performance is dramatically affected, for better or worse, by leader expectation. Positive expectations not only make people feel good, they promote confidence. And confidence, even if misplaced, results in superior performance. These studies, conducted in schools, companies, and the military, consistently demonstrate that when leaders are convinced that their teams *are* high performers, high performance is the result.

In a classic example of this type of study entitled "Pygmalion Goes to Boot Camp: Expectancy, Leadership, and Trainee Performance," published in the *Journal of Applied Psychology,* army combat command instructors were told that a number of randomly selected trainees were gifted with superior leadership potential. At the completion of the fifteen-week course, the researchers concluded that "trainees of whom instructors had been induced to expect better performance scored significantly higher on objective achievement tests, exhibited more positive attitudes, and perceived more positive leadership behavior." When the course instructors were debriefed and informed that the "superior" trainees had been selected at random, they refused to believe it.

Keep in mind that people sense your expectations for them not only through what you say but, more powerfully, by the way you look

> A great manager has a knack for making ballplayers think they are better than they think they are.
>
> —Reggie Jackson, Baseball Hall of Famer

at them, your facial expressions, and the quality of your voice. The alignment of your words with your nonverbal signals is a key to your effectiveness as a coach and leader.

After every Olympic competition, gold medal winners are interviewed by the press. A reporter usually asks, "What's the secret of your success?" And champion after champion replies, "I couldn't have done it without my coach, mom, teacher, dad, uncle, husband, boss, wife, or friend who always believed in me." You want to be the person whose belief in others changes their lives.

⁝ Give Encouragement: Catch People Doing Something Right! ⁝

When many of us were growing up, our parents, teachers, and coaches often thought they were helping us by pointing out everything we did wrong. Don't pass this approach on to the next generation. Although feedback on our mistakes is essential, it's also critical to know what we are doing that is working. So catch people doing something right. Give them accurate, appreciative feedback.

Chances are that most people in your organization and family feel unappreciated. Research suggests that to be perceived as evenhanded, you must give four positive comments for every negative comment. Catching someone doing something right and acknowledging him for it costs nothing.

Accurate, appreciative feedback elicits positive feelings, and positive feelings encourage the quest for excellence. The heart of the word "encouragement" is "courage" (from the root "cour," meaning "heart"). This quality of the heart is required if someone is to stretch beyond the fear of failure to embrace new learning. A recent extensive survey by the Gallup Organization concluded that individual productivity and organizational high performance are enhanced profoundly by a working environment characterized by the consistent communication of positive energy and encouragement.

Of course, fear and intimidation can be used to get short-term results. But in the long run, they create systemic dysfunction, what John Dewey called "compensatory maladjustment." The great champion of quality, Dr. W. Edwards Deming, emphasized the importance of "driving out fear" to create a high performance organizational system.

Go One on One: Relationships generate results and relationships are best cultivated one on one. There's truth in the aphorism that "people do not care how much you know until they know how much you care," and investing the time to meet individually is one of the best ways to show that you do. Many misunderstandings in the workplace and at home occur when people don't take the time to sit down together and work out their problems. If you are boss, supervisor, or coach, take time on a regular basis to meet one on one with your team members. You would be wise to apply this lesson also to your relationships with friends and loved ones.

Besides demonstrating your caring, one-on-one coaching is important because people learn in different ways. Some rely primarily on visual input; others prefer the auditory channel. Still others require a more hands-on kinesthetic experience. Some need an in-depth analysis of the task, while others just want the big picture. When working with an individual, find out what works best for him and communicate accordingly.

Be Patient: Remember the ebb and flow of the individual learning graph with its stages of improvement, decline, and plateaus. Seek to understand where each person is on her graph of progress and allow adequate time for the process to evolve.

Free Yourself from Ego Involvement: If you've ever witnessed a parent running onto the field to berate an umpire in the middle of a Little League game, you can appreciate the dangers of inappropriate ego involvement. If you're fully committed to helping people achieve their goals, you must avoid linking your own self-esteem to their performance. This balancing act tends to be particularly challenging because it takes great confidence to allow others appropriate time to solve problems independently without meddling and micro-managing. And the same sense of security is required to allow others to thrive and receive recognition.

∴ Ducere: Ask Questions ∴

What happens in your mind when you are asked a question? Most people find that it causes them to . . . think! So, in the great tradition of Socrates, improve your coaching effectiveness by using language that promotes a process of self-discovery.

Midwife of the Mind

Socrates, perhaps history's supreme role model for great teaching, actually insisted that he was *not* a teacher. Rather, he referred to himself as a "midwife of the mind," dedicated to helping others bring forth their healthiest mental progeny. His famed Socratic method was to ask questions—questions which provoked, challenged, and guided people to develop their own best ideas. My friend Ron Gross, author of *Socrates' Way*, points out that "As a coach, Socrates exemplified the principles in this chapter: he worked one on one, put his ego aside, and was patient; he used humor; he was encouraging— but he demanded excellence. He's a great role model for bringing out the best in others."

The word *education* comes from the root "ducere," which means "to draw along" or "to lead." But many of us were schooled as though "ducere" meant "to stuff in." If we are not careful, we can find ourselves applying this old model when leading and coaching others.

In the spirit of the real root of education, ask questions that lead people to find things out for themselves. Gerry Kirk, managing director of Merck's Central American operation, coordinates a team of representatives from each of the seven countries for which he is responsible. Kirk says, "Success in this job begins with asking people the right questions." He emphasizes that asking questions allows him to stay informed while helping him provide effective guidance. He adds, "Although the traditional culture here was 'command and control,' I'm convinced that if I had just continued telling people what to do, as expected, we wouldn't have been able to change the historical performance trends and, thus, to break away from the competition. By continuous questioning and careful listening, I can very effectively maintain all of the many balls we have in the air at once. I use questions to help my people discover things for themselves, thereby engendering a greater feeling of self-confidence, professional pride, and true empowerment. Over the course of the years, the result has been a 'culture shift' to a more cooperative, collaborative model and, most importantly, an across-the-board improvement in our business."

∴ Feed the Success Mechanism by Setting SMART Goals and Offering SMART Feedback: ∴

Help every member of your team establish vivid, compelling, multisensory images of their goals.

Make goals SMART:

S—Specific: Define exactly what you want to accomplish, in detail.
M—Measurable: Decide how you will measure your progress, and, most important, how you will know that you have achieved your goal.
A—Accountability: Make a full commitment to be personally responsible for achieving your goal. When setting goals in a team, be certain that accountability is clear.

R—*Realistic and Relevant:* Set goals that are ambitious but achievable. Check that your goals are relevant to your overall purpose and values.

T—*Timeline:* Create a clear timeline for the achievement of your goals.

Encourage your team to write down and articulate their SMART goals, and to review them regularly.

Once you all clearly agree on your goals, you can apply SMART feedback to keep your team on track to achieve them.

S—*Specific:* Specifics are more constructive than broad generalities, and descriptions of behavior are more useful than summary judgments. To tell someone "You're insensitive to clients" or "You're a slob" is not as constructive as "You interrupted the client twice and failed to make eye contact" or "Your shirttail was hanging out and your shoes were unshined."

M—*Monitored:* The only way to measure the success of your feedback is through the results it achieves. Complete your feedback session by asking the recipient to express what she has understood. Check that her response matches your associations with your original message. Measure your effectiveness as a giver of feedback by how well she implements your advice and changes her behavior.

A—*Actionable:* To be useful, feedback must refer to a behavior that a person can change. To remind someone of something that he is powerless to change will only increase his frustration and sabotage his trust in you. For example, "John, I'm afraid that you just aren't tall enough to cut the right figure in sales meetings." Instead, try "John, let's find a way to strengthen your presence in sales meetings."

R—*Respectful:* For your feedback to be taken to heart, you must create and sustain an atmosphere of respect, rapport, and trust. If your feedback springs from empathic observation, sensitivity, and a sincere concern to guide others to fulfill their highest potential, then people will increasingly seek you out to ask for it. You can promote respect and rapport by asking people to evaluate their own strengths and weaknesses first. People are usually much more receptive to your observations when you demonstrate respect by asking for theirs. Moreover, by asking first, and listening carefully, you will usually learn something valuable that you would not otherwise have known.

T—Timely and Well Timed: Feedback is most useful when given promptly. If you want to give someone feedback on his performance at a meeting, for example, give it as soon as possible after the meeting, not a few weeks later. In addition to being timely, you want to ensure that the feedback is *well timed.* The best feedback is useless if the time or place prevents it from being digested. For example, even the most brilliant critical feedback will almost always do more harm than good if you offer it in public. Ask your team member to tell you when they'd prefer to get some feedback on their performance.

For the success mechanism to function properly, people need to compare the reality of their current performance with a clear idea of what they need to do to reach the desired goal. As a manager or coach, you are the steward of this mechanism's functioning.

Ask Your People to Teach: William Faulkner once wrote, "I don't know what I think until I've read what I've written." Frequently, we aren't aware of how much we have learned until we express it to someone else. Furthermore, teaching what we've learned compels us to integrate and incorporate our learning at a deeper level. Encouraging your team to teach others what they have learned accelerates their own path to mastery.

Be Your Own Coach: Take every opportunity to study models of excellence in managing, leading, coaching, and teaching. Incorporate the skills of the best guides and coaches you have ever met. Learn what *not* to do from your worst teachers. Then, whenever you are at an impasse in your work or personal life, when you're having a hard time keeping all the balls in the air, ask: "What would my ideal coach say?"

> It is good when the teacher becomes the student and the student becomes the teacher.
>
> —ancient Chinese wisdom

Good to Great

According to an ancient Japanese proverb, "When you have completed 95 percent of your journey you are only halfway there." The willingness to travel the last 5 percent separates the great from the very good.

⑥

Having a Ball! Bringing It All Together

———————

Juggling changed my life. After achieving my first three-ball juggulation I was hooked and decided that I wanted to juggle five balls, a feat that seemed impossible. I approached the challenge by defining and then applying the 5 Keys to High Performance Learning. I practiced day after day and dropped the balls thousands of times. Then one day, while I was standing over my couch, I threw all five balls in the air and they floated effortlessly into my hands. The five-ball pattern "just happened," and for a few cycles it continued as I looked on with wonder. Then I said to myself, "Hey, I'm doing it," and all the balls dropped immediately. Nevertheless, it was a peak experience. I realized in that moment that if I applied these principles **I could learn anything I wanted to learn.**

Before my juggling epiphany I believed, like most people, that there were things that I just couldn't learn, or things that I just wouldn't learn, because of the discomfort associated with them. For example, when I was seven years old, a counselor at summer camp threw me into the deep end of the swimming pool in a misguided effort to help me overcome my fear of the water. Besides believing that I couldn't swim, I also had "I Can'ts" about singing, drawing, and writing. Applying the 5 Keys, I learned to swim for miles and enjoy it. I learned to sing—and even performed a couple of times—and then I learned to draw and wrote an introductory guide to help others begin learning how to draw. I'm still working on learning to write, but the process has enriched my life on many levels.

In my quest for deeper understanding of relaxed concentration in the learning process, I began studying the martial art of Aikido at age thirty-five. I resolved to attain black belt rank before age forty and to reach third degree black belt before age forty-five. Aikido is the most difficult martial art to master, and its practice is an exercise in humility. Although I admit to being somewhat nervous before appearing on national television or speaking to groups of thousands of people, the butterflies in my stomach in those situations were flying in formation compared to their wild flight pattern before my first white-belt test in Aikido. As I waited on the side of the mat for my name to be called, my mouth was turning to cotton and the air in the room seemed to disappear. Then I had a thought that saved me: "Hey, you've been traveling around the world for years telling corporate executives to 'let the balls drop' and 'learn to love your mistakes.' How about applying that philosophy yourself, *now!*" Giving myself permission to fail changed everything. Suddenly I could breathe, and the test was a breeze. Nine years later I took my third degree black belt test in front of an audience of five hundred people, and after almost a decade of modeling excellence, creative visualization, and a mistake-positive attitude, it was easy to keep my neck free and my eyes soft as five younger, larger attackers came charging at me from different directions. As I evaded each attacker, I had another epiphany: It was just like juggling! Just as the five balls seemed to juggle themselves, my five attackers seemed to fall down with minimal effort on my part.

Of course the real test of these principles is in everyday life. In managing my own business and life and in consulting with organizations and coaching individuals for more than twenty-five years, juggling has proved invaluable. Most of this work involves asking questions in a way that helps clients activate their success mechanism, first, by clarifying what they want to achieve, and then by overcoming blocks to gaining accurate feedback on their progress. Of course, people are much more open to confronting the gaps between their ideals and reality when they take a mistake-positive perspective. Learning to love your mistakes takes the fear out of learning and unleashes the power of play, thereby accelerating the learning process, encouraging innovation, and making work more fun. My clients have not only learned to "focus on the throw" and "let the balls drop," but they've also been introduced to practical mind-body disciplines like the Alexander Technique and Aikido that help them stay centered in the midst of apparent chaos. **This balancing of body and mind, of equipoise and equanimity, makes all the difference in getting more done with fewer resources. The most effective leaders understand the importance of what they do *not* do. Like world-class athletes, jugglers, musicians, and Aikido practitioners, they know this secret of investing minimal effort for maximum return.**

After leading executive retreats for organizations around the world for a few years I realized that teaching individuals how to learn faster was a necessary, but not sufficient, condition for creating a learning organization. The learning organization demands that its members see the big picture (vision, strategy, leadership, values) while attending to details (mission, tactics, management, goals), just as one must attend to the whole pattern of the juggling cascade while maintaining the right relationship with each individual ball. The skills of coaching as expressed in Chapter 5 are simple, powerful keys to bridging the gaps between the details and the big picture and between individual performance and organizational excellence.

Juggling changed my life, and it can change yours too. You can, of course, derive full benefit from the application of the 5 Keys without ever picking up a juggling ball. But I strongly urge you to give it a try. You'll be amazed at how liberating, how free, and how fun it can be. And learning the art of juggling will bring you that much closer to successfully juggling all the goals, challenges, and responsibilities in your life.

In Part III I will take you, step by step, through the juggling learning process. You'll build on a series of small successes designed to nurture your confidence and enjoyment. I'll help you to overcome the most common errors on the path to three-ball mastery and then introduce you to a range of delightful tricks.

If you're already a three-ball juggler, then you will learn the secret of juggling four balls, and if you can do four I'll show you how to do five. I'll also introduce you to some of the simplest and most delightful partner juggling variations and give you some tips on performing. Get ready to have a ball.

Part II

The Art of Juggling: Expanding Your Influence with Spheres

To see a world in a grain of sand
   and heaven in a wild flower,
   hold infinity in the palm of your hand
   and eternity in an hour.
       —William Blake, "Auguries of Innocence"

Holding Infinity in the Palm of Your Hand: Learning the Basic Cascade

The basic juggling pattern is called a **cascade:** three balls moving in a horizontal figure eight. This pattern is also known as the symbol of infinity. The **infinity pattern** offers an inspiring reminder of your virtually infinite capacity to learn.

When people ask how I learned to juggle, if I don't tell them the story I shared with you in the introduction to this book, then I tell them this one: "I was walking down the street one day when I saw three balls circulating in the infinity pattern. So I stood behind them and have been there ever since."

In this chapter you'll be guided step by step to learn the infinity pattern and enter the **juggling flow state** which is akin to the experience described by William Blake in his poem "Auguries of Innocence."

As you learn to juggle, you'll be reviewing and applying the 5 Keys to High Performance Learning introduced in Part I. You'll also discover that juggling practice is a delightful way to clear your mind and promote relaxed concentration. Juggling will help you balance the two sides of your body and brain. You'll improve your hand-eye coordination and your ambidexterity. Juggling also serves as a marvelous warm-up for other activities. A few minutes of juggling practice before a round of golf or tennis, or before giving a major presentation or participating in an important meeting, will probably improve your performance. Most of all, if you stick with it, you'll discover that juggling is just plain fun.

Juggle Your Way to Fitness

Juggling practice offers a number of fitness benefits. It promotes lively muscle tone, quickened reflexes, better hand-eye coordination, and more refined balance and poise. And in the early stages, retrieving your juggling balls can provide considerable aerobic training.

As you progress, you can build upper body strength and power by juggling heavy objects. Juggling can also be combined with running ("joggling") and dancing ("jiggling") to provide aerobic benefit to the advanced student.

You'll recall the original instruction I received from my first teacher: "Take these three balls, throw them up, and don't let any of them drop!" The instructions you receive in this chapter will be more helpful and more detailed and will guarantee your success in every stage of the learning process. Let's begin by considering the ideal learning environment:

The quality of your environment is a powerful influence on your learning process. Whether you are planning a strategy or finalizing a budget, studying for an exam, learning to play the piano, or attending a seminar, you'll learn faster and more effectively with appropriate space, natural lighting, fresh air, the right equipment, and in some cases the right music. The best environment in which to learn to juggle has:

Space: You can, and eventually will, juggle anywhere. In the early stages of your juggling, however, you will want to create a supportive environment. If you are juggling indoors, select an area with high ceilings, plenty of room, and a minimum number of breakable objects.

Light: Natural sunlight is best for juggling. When this is not available, full-spectrum or incandescent lights are the best substitutes. Avoid practicing under fluorescent light, as it creates eye strain and interferes with the integration of your left and right brain hemispheres. Poor lighting can also disrupt your physical balance and disturb your perception of form and shape.

Air: Weighing in at only 2 to 3 percent of your body's weight, your brain uses more than 20 percent of your body's oxygen. So, whenever possible, juggle in a space with good ventilation and fresh air.

Music: The right music will awaken your sense of rhythm and make learning more fun. Baroque and classical music have a particularly powerful positive effect on beginning jugglers. Research indicates that this music, especially the music of Mozart, encourages the balance or coherence of the brain waves of the two hemispheres of your cerebral cortex. Jazz music is also a wonderful accompaniment to your juggling practice, especially when you're improvising new tricks. Experiment to discover the music that works best for you. If music isn't available, you may find it helpful to hum, whistle, or sing to yourself.

Equipment: Professional jugglers use lacrosse balls or special silicone juggling balls, although tennis balls or racquet balls—indeed, any balls that you can throw and catch easily and comfortably and which appeal to your senses—will be appropriate. It's best to find balls of different colors. This will make it easier for you to see each element in the juggling pattern.

Ball Management

When I first learned to juggle, the balls fell on the floor of my apartment thousands of times. When my landlord informed me that I would be evicted if this continued, I improvised by juggling over the couch in my living room. If you find yourself in a similar situation, practice your juggling beside a bed or couch so when the balls fall, they don't land on the floor.

Bean Bags: Bean bags have the apparent advantage of not bouncing when dropped, so you are less likely to break things and spend lots of time running after the balls. But they are fundamentally static and may limit your creative possibilities. Balls provide a livelier feeling in your hands, and the bouncing ball offers valuable feedback on the appropriateness of the strength and direction of your throw. As you progress, you'll find that the bounce of a fallen ball will become the inspiration for many of your new juggling tricks.

Scarves: To boost your confidence, you may wish to experiment by juggling light scarves. Scarves have the advantage of floating in the air when tossed, creating a *slow motion* juggling experience.

Juggling Clubs and Other Things: Once you know how to juggle, you can juggle just about anything as long as you can lift it, toss it, and catch it. Besides balls, juggling clubs are the most popular juggling objects. Juggling clubs are marvelous tools of the juggler's art because they are highly visible, they create a pleasant audible rhythm, and they provide a lot of kinesthetic satisfaction. Club juggling is a bit trickier than ball juggling because it requires that you spin the club as well as toss and catch it, but this is easy to work out with a little practice.

TIP: Hold the club toward its center of gravity—this makes it much easier to control.

Some other objects that are fun to juggle include cigar boxes, scarves, eggs, fruits, and basketballs.

High Performance Learning Tip

As you progress, you may decide that you'd like to perform publicly as a juggler. In that case, prepare yourself by practicing in conditions *opposite* those described above. Most performance venues, such as corporate auditoriums, conference rooms, or nightclubs, have low ceilings, bad air, glaring lights, and other distractions. Start with the best conditions and work your way down.

While studying in London in the midseventies I supplemented my income by working as a juggler at the Beefeater by the Tower, a restaurant-nightclub that hosted five hundred tourists nightly for a Henry VIII revel. In addition to performing five shows a night I was also responsible for helping to seat the guests while serving as bodyguard for the exotic dancer. Dodging the scurrying serving wenches and fending off large drunken would-be dancer-gropers while juggling a bowling ball, apple, and grape in bad light under low ceilings made all my later performance experiences seem easy.

Before You Start Juggling, Remember To:

Breathe: Monitor yourself and check that you are breathing easily. Many people hold their breath when throwing and catching the balls. Allow yourself to breathe fully and freely, occasionally allowing a deep and extended exhalation (sighing and yawning are useful). Every now and then, test the ease and freedom of your breathing by making an extended whispered *ahhhh* sound.

Access Poise: The basic juggling posture, applicable to all stages of juggling, is upright and relaxed. Place your feet shoulder-width apart. Stand at your full height. Let your shoulders rest easily on your torso, with your entire body in alignment and your head freely balanced on top. Keep your elbows close to the sides of your body. Smile.

⁛ One-Ball Juggling: Instant Success! ⁛

Start by Playing with One Ball: Take one ball and play with it. Throw the ball high; bounce it off the ground; enjoy the feeling of letting the ball drop.

Focus on the Throw and
Let Catching Take Care of Itself

Have you ever had someone toss something your way that you caught without thinking? This catching reflex is a natural ability that emerges when you are not worried about *trying* to catch. In the early stages of your juggling, keep your attention on the quality of your throws and let catching take care of itself.

Visualize the Juggler's Box: The juggler's box can be used as the framework for all your juggling. Imagine a box of space. The bottom plane is located at the level of your navel, the top plane approximately six inches above the top of your head. Your hands rest on the bottom plane of the box, relaxed and open, forearms parallel with the ground and elbows close to your body.

Balls thrown from your right hand are aimed at a point to the left of center of the top of the box. When you hit this point, the ball will land in your left hand.

Balls thrown from your left hand are aimed at a point to the right of center of the top of the box. When you hit this point, the ball will land in your right hand.

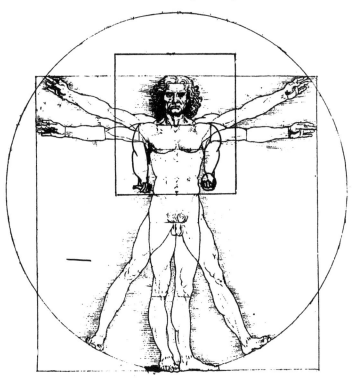

The Juggler's Box

Juggle One Ball: Throw a ball to the top of the box, letting the ball land in your other hand.

When throwing the ball, release it with minimal effort. Extend and then flex the elbow and wrist slightly, sending the ball off your fingertips to the point at the top of the box.

If your throw doesn't land near your waiting hand, just **let it drop.** Then pause. Allow a deep breath, and reinforce your mental image of where you want your throw to go.

Monitor your posture, balance, and breathing, focusing on releas-

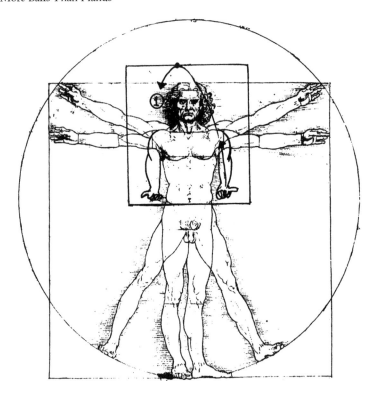

One-Ball Juggling

ing the ball with minimal effort. As you incorporate the mechanics of one-ball juggling, you will begin to discover a pleasing rhythm.

"Soft Eyes"

Softly focus your eyes at the center of the top of the box. This allows your peripheral vision to take in all the information you will need to juggle accurately. Keep your eyes *softly* focused, and your hands will automatically adjust to the appropriate receiving position. There is no need to look at your hands, as your kinesthetic sense provides a reliable guide to their location.

 Two Balls

The good news is that juggling two or three balls requires doing exactly what you have done with one, sequentially. The simple steps are:

Step 1: *Tossing and Dropping Two Balls*
Place one ball in each hand.
Throw the ball in your right hand to the appropriate point at the top of the box just as you did when juggling one ball.
As your first throw reaches its apex, throw the ball in your left hand to its corresponding destination at the top of the box. **Let both balls drop.**
If you throw the balls to their respective points at the top of the box, they will land, in staggered timing, a few inches in front of your feet.

Step 2: *Tossing Two, Catching One*
Toss the balls in the same staggered timing as step 1, only this time catch the first toss.
Let the second ball drop.

Step 3: *Tossing Two, Catching Two*
This step is identical to step 2, but now catch them both. If your tosses don't land in the general area of your hands, just **let the balls drop.** Keep your primary focus on the accuracy of your *throws,* allowing the catching to take care of itself.

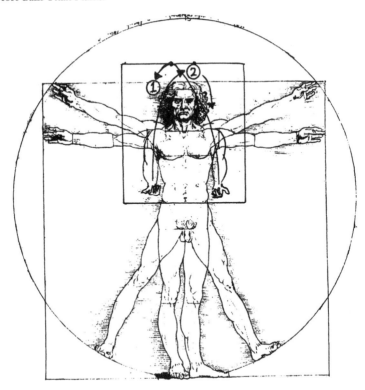

Two-Ball Juggling

After you have practiced with two balls for ten to twenty minutes, move on to the first stages of three-ball juggling even if you have not mastered two balls.

Why Try Three Before You've Mastered Two?

You might ask: "How can I possibly do three when I haven't mastered two?" **By stretching yourself beyond your perceived level of competence, you will accelerate your**

development of competence. This general learning principle is reflected perfectly in making the leap from two to three balls. After attempting three balls and stretching yourself beyond your apparent limits, two balls will seem much easier.

As high performance coaches Tony Schwartz and Jim Loehr advise in *The Power of Full Engagement,* "To build capacity, we must systemically expose ourselves to *more* stress—followed by adequate recovery. Challenging a muscle past its current limits prompts a phenomenon knows as *supercompensation.* Faced with a demand that exceeds our current capacity, the body responds by building more muscle fibers in anticipation of the next stimulus. We grow at all levels by expending energy beyond our normal limits, and then recovering. The same is true, we have found, of 'muscles' at all levels—emotional, mental and spiritual."

⁘ Three-Ball Juggling: Your First Juggulation ⁘

Step 1: *Throwing and Dropping Three Balls*

Take two balls in one hand, one ball in the other hand. **The hand with two balls will always be the one with which you start.**

Throw the first ball to its point at the top of the box. As it reaches its apex, throw the second ball to its point at the top of the box. As the *second* ball reaches its apex, throw the *third* ball to its point at the top of the box (the same place you aimed your first throw). **Let each ball drop.**

Practice releasing the balls in a fluid rhythm without even thinking of catching. Focus on where you want the balls to go (the points at the top of the box) and enjoy letting them drop. Continue experimenting with your rhythm until you are dropping all three balls with panache.

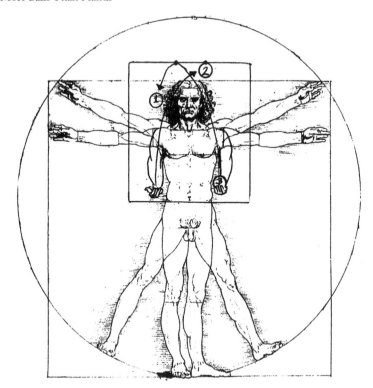

Three-Ball Juggling

Step 2: *Tossing Three, Catching One*

Throw the three balls up as in step 1. This time, allow the first ball to land in your opposite hand. Let the other two drop.

Step 3: *Tossing Three, Catching Two*

Throw the three balls as in step 2, but this time, allow the *first and second* balls to land in your hands, while letting the third drop.

You will notice that when the two balls land in your hands, there is only one ball left in the air.

Step 4: *Your First Juggulation: Tossing Three, Catching Three*

Throw the three balls as in the previous steps, catching them in sequence as they land in the vicinity of your hands. When you have accomplished this, **the tossing and catching of all three balls,** you will have achieved your first juggulation. Celebrate.

High Performance Learning Tip

You can accelerate your progress in juggling or any other learning task by beginning with an intensive practice session. New learning can be compared with the flight of a rocket: the greatest energy is required during takeoff. If you want to learn a new language, for example, you will find that if you begin with a few days of total immersion, all your subsequent efforts will yield greater results. Once you've launched your new endeavor, experiment with the times of day in which you learn best. Some people learn best first thing in the morning while others do better in the late afternoon. Experiment with your learning biorhythms and design your practice schedule accordingly.

⋮⋮ Multiple Juggulation ⋮⋮

Next, you simply continue throwing the balls. Keep the primary focus of your attention on continuing to *throw,* without worrying about catching.

Your fourth throw will be the same ball that you started with, but this time you will be throwing it with the opposite hand because that is where it will have landed after you threw it the first time. (Remember to make this first/fourth ball a different color, so that you can immediately recognize it as the ball that you have to throw.)

At this stage, it's useful to go back to the image of the box, checking the height, trajectory, and timing of your throws. Be sure that your shoulders haven't crept up to your ears, and that you're breathing freely.

Now simply instruct yourself to "throw, throw, throw, throw, throw, throw," directing the balls to the points at the top of the box. Let the catching take care of itself and enjoy dropping the balls when you do. Seek a fluid, easy rhythm.

If you find yourself getting stuck or frustrated: Pause, exhale, and in your mind's eye, picture where you want the balls to go.

If you're still stuck, return for a minute or two to an earlier stage of the process (tossing three and dropping three, or perhaps some one-ball practice). Focus on the direction and timing of your throws and your own poise. As your throwing accuracy improves, the balls will land in your hands. No matter what happens or how fast you progress, remember that juggling—including dropping the balls— should be practiced in a spirit of fun and joy.

> He who binds to himself a joy
> Does the winged life destroy;
> But he who kisses the joy as it flies
> Lives in eternity's sunrise.
>
> —William Blake,
> "Several Questions Answered"

 Juggling Toward Infinity

Once you have completed your first juggulation, you may wish to set yourself a progressive series of goals toward infinity such as:

- 4 accurate throws
- 5 accurate throws

- 6 accurate throws, 2 continuous juggulations (When you attain 6 throws—two 3-ball circuits—you will have exceeded the boundary of static juggulation, entering the realm of the juggling flow state)
  - 9 throws (3 complete continuous juggulations)
  - 21 throws (7 complete continuous juggulations)
  - 100 throws (33.3 complete continuous juggulations)
  - 1,000 throws (333.3 complete continuous juggulations)

At this point, the thrill of counting the number of your accurate throws may begin to wane. Instead, you can set time-measured goals for maintaining the juggling flow state (thirty seconds, a minute, five minutes, and then whatever personal marathon goals you choose).

You can take your "juggling pulse" by timing yourself for a minute, counting the number of complete continuous juggulations (CCJs). In this way, you can keep an idea of how many CCJs you are completing in the time you maintain the juggling flow state.

If you want a more formal grading system, turn to the appendix, "Milestones to Infinity: The Master Juggler Grid," which will help you measure your progress toward your jugglerian black belt.

Juggling in the Mind's Eye

If you've never juggled before, then chances are that in your mind's eye you start with a very vague picture of juggling. Perhaps you imagine the balls flying, and probably dropping, from your hands. As you read and practice the exercises in this section, your mental image of juggling will become clearer and more complete. As you practice and receive feedback, your internal picture of juggling will evolve. As your internal picture evolves, your performance will improve.

⫶ Solving the Classic Problems ⫶

In every stage of learning to juggle, you will encounter challenges to your ability to maintain the juggling flow state. Here are some of the classic problems:

Problems? Have a Ball!

The word *problem* comes from the roots "pro," meaning *forward,* and "ballein," meaning *to throw* or *drive* (the same root as *ball*). The verb *solve* comes from the root "solvere," which means *to loosen, release,* or *set free.* Webster defines a *problem* as "a question proposed for solution or consideration." So *problem solving* is the process of proposing and considering questions in a way that throws or drives us forward toward greater freedom.

Colliding Balls

Problem: The balls bang into one another.

Solution: Although in your advanced juggling you may wish to bounce the balls together in space as a trick, you'll need to make an adjustment if it is happening unintentionally.

Colliding balls are caused either by an overly narrow trajectory (throwing the balls straight up), or by throwing a ball before the previous throw has reached its apex (throwing the second ball too soon).

To ensure the appropriate trajectory, check your throws. Make sure:

1. that the first ball is thrown to the appropriate point at the top of the box, and

2. that the second ball is thrown to its appropriate point at the top of the box, in such a way as to go *underneath the flight path of the first ball.*

To prevent premature throwing, wait until the first throw has reached its apex *before* releasing the next ball.

Showering Instead of Cascading

Problem: The balls are passed directly from one hand to the other along the lower plane of the box.

This pattern, known as showering, is a standard juggling pattern. It tends, however, to exacerbate body asymmetry and to limit the freedom and flexibility in your juggling and is thus inappropriate until you have mastered the three-ball cascade.

Solution: Throw the first ball to the top of the box and let it drop. Pause for a moment. Visualize where you want the second throw to go. When you're confident that you can throw the second ball to its appropriate apex, do so.

When you succeed in throwing the balls accurately with this pause, decrease the time between throws until the cascade flows naturally.

Asymmetrical Throwing

Problem: One hand seems to have a mind of its own (usually your nondominant hand) and is consistently throwing the balls out of the box and out of range of your other hand.

Solution: Observe the energy and direction of the errant throw. Refine your focus on the dimensions of the box and on where, specifically, you want the balls to go in space.

If the challenge persists, go back to one-ball practice for a few minutes, focusing on the symmetry of your tosses. This will eventually transfer to your three-ball juggling.

You can also often correct asymmetrical throwing by starting your juggling with your non-dominant hand and bringing extra attention to the quality of the throws from that hand.

Getting Stuck at the End of the First Juggulation

Problem: You've completed your first juggulation and you don't know how to continue.

Solution: Having achieved your first juggulation, celebrate and be prepared to move on. The secret is to keep the emphasis on *throwing*. In order to progress, you must be willing to start dropping the balls again, raising yourself to a higher level of chaos.

As you juggle, count aloud with each toss—"one, two, three." During your second juggulation, instead of shouting "four, five, six," shout out "throw, throw, throw," tossing a ball with every shout. Keep your attention on throwing and enjoy the process of throwing and dropping or catching the balls.

Progressive Acceleration: Being Led Around by the Balls

Problem: A fanatical desire to catch every ball thrown, characterized by excessive reaching, grabbing, and lunging, with accompanying body tension and general distress. It's caused by the compulsion to grasp prematurely for results (catching), rather than attending to the process (throwing, breathing).

Solution: Juggling while facing a wall will prevent you from lunging forward. You can also walk backward while practicing, which helps you break your habit of reaching forward. The essential solution, however, is to maintain your primary focus on the quality and direction of your throws within the box. Refocus your attention on throwing the balls to the *top* of the box while keeping your hands at the *bottom* plane of the box. To access the appropriate sense of timing and dimension, you may also find it useful to imagine that you are juggling underwater or on the moon. Allow deep exhalations, exaggerate the height of your throws, and let the balls come to you. Remember, if you focus on the throw and your own poise, the balls will land in the same place consistently and you will have plenty of space and time available.

By now you will see that many of these challenges represent plateaus and downward movements in your individual graph of progress. But now you know that these are integral parts of the learning process and that if you persevere with the application of the 5 Keys of the high performance learner, your success will be inevitable.

High Performance Learning Tip

Have you ever met a basketball player who would leave the court after having missed his last shot? Hoopsters understand instinctively the importance of a positive **recency effect.** The recency effect is a phenomenon discovered by psychological researchers. It states that you are more likely to remember things that happen at the end of a learning session. When you finish on a high note, your strongest memory, until your next practice session, will be of success. This will help you build the confidence that nurtures a positive learning cycle. So, whether just before a break or at the end of a practice session, finish at a high point.

Beyond Infinity: Advanced Juggling

The basic three-ball cascade provides the background for mastery of all advanced juggling tricks. You will probably discover that as you become more comfortable with your three-ball cascade, you will be able to lower the height of your throws. As you try the tricks in this chapter, you will again want to take advantage of the full dimensions of the juggler's box.

Expanding Your Kinesphere

The level of freedom you have in experimenting with new tricks will be determined by the effortlessness with which you can perform the three-ball cascade. One way to cultivate effortlessness in your three-ball cascade as well as to learn a very impressive advanced juggling trick is to practice with your eyes closed. By practicing the three-ball cascade with your eyes closed, you develop much greater dependence on your kinesthetic sense; you begin to develop a sense of the **kinesphere,** the area of space around your body in which most of your juggling tricks will take place. This will help you with your other advanced tricks.

⚬ Warm-up Activities ⚬

In addition to refining your three-ball cascade, there are a number of warm-up activities that will prepare you for advanced juggling.

Perhaps the most important warm-up is simply to **play with the balls.** Practice throwing them high, letting them bounce, catching a ball off a bounce, throwing it off various parts of your body: knees, arms, feet, head. Experiment with a multitude of creative variations. These playful experiments with one, two, or three balls will form the basis of most of the advanced tricks you will be learning.

Another useful warm-up exercise is to juggle **two in one hand.** Take two balls in one hand, pick a point just outside the top of the corner of the box, and throw the first ball to that point; when that ball reaches its apex, throw the second ball. You make little circles with your hand, throwing the ball *away* from the center of your body. After you throw and catch two balls with one hand, you will have completed your first two-ball juggulation.

This two-in-one practice is an essential element of many advanced juggling tricks. It will also form the basis for four-ball juggling. Be sure to practice the two-in-one juggling with both hands equally. When you become comfortable throwing the ball in a circular pattern away from the center of your body, you can experiment with throwing the balls in *toward* your body and straight up and down.

Another warm-up exercise for advanced tricks is the **over-under exercise.** The first part of this exercise is called "suspender straps." In this exercise, you take a ball with your *right hand* and, behind your back, throw it up over your *left shoulder* to the front so it lands in your left hand. Then, with your *left hand* behind your back, throw the ball over your *right shoulder,* letting it land in your right hand. See the suspenders? Go back and forth over alternate shoulders, letting the ball land in alternate hands, until you are comfortable throwing the ball behind your back.

When you have mastered that, try the second part of the exercise.

Take the ball in your right hand and throw it under your right *leg,* catching it in your left hand. Do that back and forth. You can then try four throws under each leg, then four throws over each *shoulder.* Repeat with two throws under each leg, two throws over each shoulder. Then try one throw under each leg and one throw over each shoulder.

Next, experiment with throwing over your shoulder and catching behind your back. Improvise from there.

Besides preparing you for tricks you will soon learn, this over-under exercise is also an excellent way to enliven your kinesthetic sensitivity. As you practice the over-under exercise, you develop greater awareness of your whole body and the space that surrounds it.

 Advanced Tricks

TIP: In learning these advanced tricks, it's especially useful to have one odd-colored ball.

Shoot the Moon: Start by juggling three balls in the basic cascade. When the odd-colored ball comes to your right hand, throw it up the middle, beyond the top of the box; pause for a moment while holding the other two, and let the high toss come down in your left hand. You will have to throw the ball in your left hand up to the top of the box just before your high toss lands in your hand. Then continue your juggling cascade. Once you get comfortable with the high toss, you can experiment with throwing the ball higher and higher, waiting for it to come down. Although it is an easy trick, it will delight you and your audience.

Experiment with variations such as throwing the ball up high and doing a pirouette before letting it land in your opposite hand; doing a somersault, clapping your hands one, two, three, or four times; jumping up and down; and generally playing around while you wait for the ball to come down. Be sure to practice initiating this trick, and all your tricks, with each hand.

After you become comfortable throwing one ball "toward the moon," you can experiment throwing two of the balls out of your cascade into a high toss in succession (with any one of the variations previously mentioned). Then you can do the three-ball moonshot, tossing all three balls beyond the top of the box in succession. Experiment by throwing them higher and higher, pirouetting, somersaulting, or clapping as you wait for them to return from orbit.

Dropping the Balls: This is a trick you will inadvertently do many times. It's worth practicing consciously, both because it can be fun to perform and because it hones your reflexes so that when you *do* drop inadvertently, you can pick the ball(s) up and continue with your cascade.

In the basic one-ball drop, when your odd-colored ball comes to the hand of your choice, throw it up and let it drop, holding on to the other two and waiting for the odd ball to bounce back up to you. As it bounces up, you release the ball in the hand with which you are going to catch the dropped ball and incorporate it back into your cascade. After you are comfortable dropping one ball, drop two, then three. You can apply many of the same variations you did while shooting for the moon: pirouettes, handclaps, and so on.

The Reverse Infinity Series: The Reverse Infinity Series (also known as the Reverse Cascade Series) provides a whole juggling show in itself. It is a simple, elegant, and enjoyable trick to practice and perform.

When the odd-colored ball reaches the hand of your choice, you will throw it over the top of your juggling pattern. Practice throwing the same ball over the top of your pattern every time it comes to the hand of your choice. When you have become comfortable throwing every third ball over the top, experiment throwing every *other* ball that lands in the given hand over the top of the pattern, and then *every* ball over the top of the pattern. When you are comfortable doing this from one side, try the same thing from the other side.

If you started throwing the balls over the top with your right hand, then practice the Reverse Infinity Series starting with your left hand. Every time the odd-colored ball lands in your left hand, throw it over the top of the pattern. Start with every third throw, then every second ball that comes to your left hand will go over the top, and then *every* ball that comes to your left hand will go over the top. Once you are comfortable throwing every ball with your right hand over the top, and every ball with your left hand over the top, combine those two exercises. Whenever a ball lands in either your left or right hand, simply throw it over the top and you will be performing a reverse cascade.

A nice variation on the Reverse Infinity Series is to switch back and forth between your regular cascade and your reverse cascade five or six times, creating a delightful "inside-out" visual effect. Although it is simple and easy, this trick has a hypnotic effect on people.

The Fountain: The Fountain begins in the same way as Shoot the Moon. Take one ball from your left hand and throw it up the middle of the box to a point approximately two feet above the top of the box. As that ball reaches its apex, take the other two balls and simultaneously toss them over the top of the box so that they cross in midair. While those two balls are crossing in midair and you are waiting for them to come down, your first toss will be plummeting to earth. Move a hand into the center, catch that ball, and flip it back up. Move your hands back out in time to catch the two balls that have crossed over. As those two balls land in your hands, you'll still have the one ball in the air that you tossed up the center. Incorporate it into your basic cascade, and you've just completed your first Fountain.

Just as you did with the basic three-ball pattern, you will probably find it much easier to break this trick (and perhaps some of the earlier tricks) into their simplest elements:

- First, throw the ball up the center.
- Then, cross the two over the top, and let them drop while catching your central toss.
- Then, catch and retoss your central ball so that the crossing balls can land in your hands.

Break all of these advanced tricks into simple elements, focusing, as you have throughout, on letting the balls drop into your hands, or not, as the case may be.

Body Bounces: There are as many body bounces as there are body parts. The most basic body bounce tricks are the Arm Bounce, the Thigh Bounce, and the Head Bounce.

For the Arm Bounce, take your odd ball and throw it so that it lands on any part of your arm, flick your arm against the ball to knock it back up toward the top of the box, and then reincorporate it into your juggling rhythm. The same holds true for the other body parts. For the Thigh Bounce, drop the ball on your thigh, kick it up to the top of the box, and carry on from there. For the Head Bounce, do not use very heavy balls. Other possible variations on this trick are to bounce the ball off your calf muscle, your foot, your wrist, your elbow, or any other body part you choose. To make this trick easier, aim to release the ball as near as possible to the body part in question.

The Behind-the-Back Trick: The Behind-the-Back Trick is a classic crowd pleaser and a mark of a truly advanced juggler. The over-and-under warm-up provides the key to the Behind-the-Back Trick (and the Under-the-Leg Trick which you'll learn next).

When the odd ball lands in your right hand, swing your right hand behind your back and throw the ball over your left shoulder so that it lands in your left hand. You'll probably find that it's best to begin practicing by throwing the ball behind your back over your shoulder and letting it drop. At first, don't even think about trying to catch the ball from behind your back. Instead, focus on making an easy throw behind your back over your shoulder. With practice, you'll develop more control over that throw so that it begins to land near your opposite hand. As you become comfortable throwing the ball behind your back, you can catch it with your opposite hand, reincorporating it into your juggling rhythm. Be sure to practice the Behind-the-Back Trick with each hand over the opposite shoulder.

An *ultra*-advanced trick is to throw each of the balls, one hand after the other, behind your back in a continuous rhythm.

The Under-the-Leg Trick: When your odd ball lands in your right hand, throw it under your right leg up toward the top of the box. At first you'll want to focus just on throwing the ball successfully under your leg, without thinking about catching it. As you become comfortable throwing the ball under the leg up to the top of the box, you can let it land in your opposite hand and incorporate it into your basic juggling pattern. Again, be sure to practice this trick under *both* legs. You can build from there, throwing every third ball under your leg until you reach the point where you can throw each ball under your leg with either hand.

The Famous Apple-Eating Trick: This is one of *the* classic advanced juggling tricks. When you tell people that you are a juggler, they'll often ask, "Did you see that guy on TV who eats an apple while he juggles?" To which you can reply, "Yes, that seems really difficult," and then whip out your own apple and go to town.

The secret to the Famous Apple-Eating Trick is to be able to juggle with two balls in one hand comfortably. The simplest way to do the trick is to take two balls and an apple (McIntosh are best because they are relatively soft) and juggle them in the cascade pattern, then break out of your cascade pattern into a two-ball juggle with one hand. Hold the apple in your other hand and take a bite out of it (quickly), then reincorporate it into your cascade (be sure to bite the apple, not one of the balls!).

When it reaches the hand from which you originally chomped it, take another bite, again juggling the other two balls in your opposite hand. To make this trick effective, accelerate the pace at which you take bites of the apple, stuffing as much of it into your mouth as you possibly can and keep going until you have eaten just about the whole apple, at which point you plunge the core into your mouth, hold it there, raise your arms over your head, and take a bow with apple juice dripping down your chin, to the wild applause of your audience. It works every time.

Four Balls: The basic four-ball pattern involves juggling two balls in each hand at the same time:

- Practice the two-in-one exercise described in the basic warm-up.
- Juggle two balls in one hand away from the center of your body while looking straight ahead. When you are comfortable juggling two balls in each hand separately, you can . . .
- Combine them so that you are juggling two balls in each hand at the same time.

Voilà! You're juggling four balls. The secret is to move from simultaneous tosses to staggered timing of your throws, thereby creating the illusion that the four balls are crossing over. Once you have this pattern going, you can begin to experiment with variations on this basic four-ball theme.

The Five-Ball Cascade: Juggling five balls involves the same pattern as three, only with two more balls. Begin with three balls in one hand, two balls in the other. At first, practice simply throwing all five balls up to the top of the box in staggered timing (don't even think about catching them). You'll need to raise the top of your box a foot or so for five balls. Let the balls drop just as you did in learning three balls.

Keep practicing the release of the five balls as smoothly as you can and then begin experimenting with letting one ball land in your hand, letting two balls land in your hand, then three, four, five, and so on.

⁖ Building Your Own Routine ⁖

As you begin learning tricks, you will naturally start to think about how to best combine them. Create a pattern in which one trick flows into another in a way that seems beautiful to you. When building your routine, note the *feel* of one trick as it flows into another and seek the most delicious feeling of flow. Once you develop a basic sequence of tricks, practice it regularly until it becomes second nature. For performance purposes, you will want to have a "grooved" routine as a framework for your improvisations.

Of course, sometimes you will want to practice by just fooling around and having your own juggling jam session. This kind of practice is fun and helps you discover new patterns. Your best tricks are usually created in moments of spontaneous joy emerging out of playful, childlike experimentation. You can then integrate your innovations into your groove.

As you create and groove your routine, you may wish to begin performing. Before unleashing your juggling talents on the public, practice under challenging conditions: poor lighting, loud noises, a strong breeze. When you can easily adapt to a variety of distractions, you are ready for the big time.

When you do perform:

- Maintain your poise
- Keep contact with your audience
- Enjoy yourself

By enjoying your juggling (not worrying about mistakes) and following the above tips, you will be guaranteed a successful and entertaining performance. And if you apply the 5 Keys of the high performance learner in your practice, then your main challenge will be trying to make your tricks look difficult.

High Performance Learning Tip

Make consideration of poise and relaxed concentration a part of all your visualizations for all your juggling and other learning activities.

Check yourself while juggling in the mirror or video screen. Observe the various parts of your body as you juggle—especially the head, neck and shoulders—gently allowing each part to release in coordination with a general sense of expansion and upward flow through your entire being.

As you juggle, ask yourself:

"What could be easier?"

"What could be lighter?"

"What could be more fluid?"

. . . and let your body answer.

---

⑨

Infinite Connections:
Juggling with Colleagues, Friends, and Family

One of the most satisfying results of mastering the basic three-ball cascade is that with just a few minor adjustments, you can juggle with partners. Your partner juggling options are vast. In this chapter, you'll learn a few of the simplest and most enjoyable.

The Embrace: Stand side by side with your partner, facing in the same direction. Put an arm loosely around each other, leaving one free arm each. Now the *two* of you are the equivalent of *one* juggler. Begin by tossing one ball back and forth, then go on to the two-ball pattern, following the same instructions as you would if you were juggling two balls on your own. The real fun begins when you juggle three. One of you will start with two balls, the other with one ball. The person with two balls throws one up to the top of the box you have created between you. When it reaches its apex, the person with one ball throws it across, and you're on your way to juggling three balls using two hands and two bodies. Once you've got the cascade going, you can do most of the tricks mentioned in the last chapter and make up your own new tricks.

Front Stealing: Your partner stands opposite you juggling three balls in the basic cascade. Watch the three-ball pattern carefully and pick out the odd ball. Say to yourself, "When the odd ball leaves my partner's right hand and comes up to the top of the box, I will put my right hand underneath it just as it reaches its apex." Practice stealing one ball out of your partner's cascade.

After you have the first ball landing easily in your hand, you can practice taking the first ball with one hand and the second ball—as it reaches its apex—with your other hand. When you have taken the first ball with one hand and the second ball with your other hand, you'll notice that the third ball, which your partner has just thrown up, is between the two balls you are holding. Treat your partner's last throw as your first toss, then continue juggling with all three balls.

You will have just "stolen" the balls. Your partner will then steal them from you in the same manner, and you can go back and forth. The key to making this trick effective is that when you are the juggler, continue moving your hands as normal, as if the balls were not being taken. This creates a surprising and delightful visual effect.

Passing Routines: This passing routine is based on the same pattern that we followed when learning the Reverse Cascade Series. Instead of throwing every third ball over the top, then every other ball over the top, then every ball over the top, you are going to throw them across to your partner in the same rhythm.

Begin by facing your partner, each with two balls in your right hand and one in your left. Facing each other, you both raise your hands, lower them, and begin juggling at the same moment. When the single (odd) ball, which was originally in your left hand, lands in your right hand, it will be ready to become your fourth toss, and you throw it across to your partner. Each time the original odd ball returns to your right hand, you throw it across to your partner again.

If you throw the ball accurately and gently to your partner's hand and your partner throws similarly to your hand, you will not have to worry about catching. After you have succeeded in throwing to each other ten times, you can then switch to throwing *every other* ball across to your partner.

When you have done that ten times, you can throw *every* ball across to your partner. The faster the rhythm becomes, the more important it is to focus on the throw. If you remain focused on the throws, the balls will keep landing in your hands.

High Performance Learning Tip

When throwing a ball to your partner in a passing routine, toss the ball in a gentle arc so it lands softly in your partner's hand. Never throw the ball *at* your partner, always *to* your partner. Be sensitive to your partner's style and play to his strengths. Always make your partner look good. Think of yourselves as one. Then apply this approach to teamwork to all your relationships at work and at home.

Afterword: It's All About Balance

Juggling is a universal language of joy. If you apply the steps in Part II and actually learn to juggle, you'll know a secret to delight every child and to bring out the child in every adult. In Japan you'll be a **tejina-shi,** in China a **shua-chiou ren,** in Russia, Germany, and France a **jongleur,** in Italy a **giocoliere,** in Latin America and Spain a **malabarista,** and in Indonesia a **pemain sunglap.** As you develop your influence with spheres, you'll expand your sphere of influence.

The September 18, 2002, edition of *Newsweek* reported that the influential head of Shell Oil's internal think tank, the group responsible for scenario planning over the next twenty years, had hired a juggler to perform at their brainstorming sessions. The group includes some of Shell's sharpest minds. They are exposed to juggling at their meetings because it serves as a reminder of the creative, playful, and systems-oriented thinking they must do to prepare for the unexpected. As you become more proficient in juggling, you won't have to hire someone to juggle at your brainstorming sessions—you'll be able to do it yourself.

But even if you never toss a ball into the air, the juggling metaphor can serve as an inspiring reminder of the secret of life. Is there one word that expresses that secret? Yes. The word is *balance.*

What makes a wine outstanding? Luscious fruit and supple tannin in delicious balance. What's the way to personal enlightenment? Balancing mind, body, emotion, and spirit. What makes an organization great? Vision, mission, and values in balance with strategy, tactics, and execution.

Balance is the secret of life, and dynamism—an ever-changing process of adjustment, compensation, and coordination—is the secret of balance. The universe breathes. It juggles. Electrons dance around the nucleus of an atom and galaxies swirl in a pulsating universe. Tides roll in and out, the sun rises and sets, we laugh and we cry, we are born and we die.

This universal balance is expressed in the ancient Chinese symbol of yin and yang and in the smile of Leonardo da Vinci's Mona Lisa (and his wonderful drawing of the Vitruvian man, also known as the Canon of Proportion). Architecture, music, painting, and poetry all seek to express various dimensions of nature's balance. In a simple, immediate way, the metaphor and practice of juggling align us with this essential universal rhythm, echoing a pattern that links us with all creation and resonates with our deepest selves.

My wish for you is that you will apply the juggling metaphor and the 5 Keys to High Performance Learning to help you find the balance that we all seek, in your life, every day.

APPENDIX

Milestones to Infinity: The Master Juggler Grid

Formal ranking grids are used in a wide range of pursuits, from piano playing to chess and the martial arts. This grid is modeled on the ranking system used in the Japanese martial art of Aikido. Use it to measure your progress.

10th level—Juggling one ball ten times back and forth from hand to hand.

9th level—Throwing two balls to the appropriate points at the top of the box in staggered timing and letting them drop; throwing two and catching one; throwing two and catching both—a two-ball juggulation.

8th level—Ten juggulations with two balls.

7th level—Throwing three balls to the appropriate points at the top of the box and letting them all drop. Throwing three and catching one. Throwing three and catching two. Throwing three and catching three—your first three-ball juggulation.

6th level—Three complete, continuous juggulations.

5th level—Ten complete, continuous juggulations. Successful completion of one Shoot the Moon. One two-balls-in-one-hand juggulation with each hand.

4th level—Thirty-three and one-third complete, continuous three-ball juggulations (one hundred throws). One ball over the top from either side, three times continuously. Five one-hand juggulations with two balls (ten throws) with each hand individually.

3rd level—One hundred complete, continuous juggulations (three hundred throws). One complete, continuous Reverse Infinity Series. Three Fountains in a continuous series of juggulations. Twenty one-hand juggulations with two balls (forty throws) with each hand individually. Over-under exercise with one ball, ten times.

2nd level—Three hundred thirty-three and one-third complete, continuous juggulations (one thousand throws). The Behind-the-Back Trick, in the flow of a juggulation, with either hand. One hundred one-hand juggulations with two balls (two hundred throws) with each hand individually. Body Bounce Trick, in the flow of a juggulation, on the body part of your choice. Throwing a ball over your shoulder and catching it behind your back—ten times on each side.

1st level—All of the previous requirements, with a demonstrable improvement in poise, rhythm, and flow. The Behind-the-Back Trick, in the flow of a juggulation, with both hands, consecutively. The Over-the-Shoulder Trick, in the flow, with both hands, consecutively. One four-ball juggulation. One-minute juggling routine incorporating at least four different tricks, including one created by the juggler.

Black belt—All of the previous requirements, with a demonstrable improvement in poise, rhythm, and flow. Four-ball juggling for thirty seconds, continuously (approximately twenty-five juggulations). One five-ball juggulation. Two-minute, three-ball routine incorporating at least eight different tricks, including three created by the juggler.

2nd degree black belt—All of the previous requirements, with a demonstrable improvement in poise, rhythm, and flow. Four-ball juggling routine for one minute incorporating three different tricks. Five-ball juggling for three juggulations, continuously. Three balls in one hand, two juggulations.

3rd degree black belt—All of the previous requirements, with a demonstrable improvement in poise, rhythm, and flow. Four-ball juggling routine for two minutes incorporating six different tricks. Five-ball juggling for twenty seconds, continuously. One six-ball juggulation. Smooth seven-ball drop!

RECOMMENDED READING

Bennis, Warren. *On Becoming a Leader.* New York: Addison-Wesley Publishing Co., Inc., 1989. Bennis's profiles of twenty-eight leaders show that the ability to bounce back after dropping the balls is a key to success.

Buzan, Tony. *The Mind Map Book: Radiant Thinking.* London: BBC Books, 1993. Buzan's masterpiece, the ultimate guide to mind mapping.

Collins, Jim. *Good to Great.* New York, HarperCollins, 2001. Deservedly influential.

Covey, Stephen. *The 7 Habits of Highly Effective People.* New York: Simon & Schuster, Inc., 1989. Systematized common sense.

Farson, Richard, and Ralph Keyes. *Whoever Makes the Most Mistakes Wins.* New York: The Free Press, 2002. The definitive guide to what the authors deem the "postfailure era."

Fincher, Jack. *Lefties: The Origin and Consequences of Being Left-Handed.* New York: Putnam, 1977. An amusing and well-researched overview of the relationship between hand and brain.

Fuller, Buckminster. *Critical Path.* New York: St. Martin's Press, 1981. Fuller emphasized that the vast potential of the brain is released through the process of trial and error.

Gallwey, W. Timothy. *The Inner Game of Tennis.* London: Jonathan Cape Ltd., 1975. Accessible, athletic Zen.

Gelb, Michael. *Present Yourself!* Rolling Estates, CA: Jalmar Press, 1988. An *Elements of Style* for creative speakers.

———. *Body Learning: An Introduction to the Alexander Technique,* 3rd ed. London: Aurum Press, 1994. *Publishers Weekly* called this the most lucid book on the subject.

———. *How to Think Like Leonardo da Vinci: Seven Steps to Genius*

Every Day. New York: Dell Publishing, 1998. Leonardo was a juggler!

———. *Discover Your Genius: How to Think Like History's Ten Most Revolutionary Minds.* New York: HarperCollins, 2002. Ten of history's great role models for developing your creativity and learning power.

———. *The New Mind Map.* New York: High Performance Learning Press, 2002. A road map for your mind.

Gross, Ron. *Socrates' Way: Seven Master Keys to Using Your Mind to the Utmost.* New York: Tarcher, 2002. Brings history's greatest coach to life (www.socratesway.com).

Herrigel, Eugen. *Zen in the Art of Archery.* New York: Vintage Books, 1971. The original Zen application book, it offers penetrating insights into attaining excellence in any discipline.

Jones, Frank Pierce. *Body Awareness in Action: A Study of the Alexander Technique.* New York: Schocken Books, 1976. This excellent book includes an extensive discussion of Jones's groundbreaking scientific study of the Alexander Technique, including Jones's work on the startle pattern.

Lao-tzu. Tao-te Ching: A New English Version with Foreword and Notes by Stephen Mitchell. New York: Harper & Row, 1988. The Bible of nondoing and unlearning.

Leonard, George. *Mastery.* New York: Dutton, 1991. An eloquent invitation to a lifetime of learning.

Samuels, M., and N. Samuels. *Seeing with the Mind's Eye.* New York: Random House, 1976. This comprehensive work provides fascinating information on the history and uses of visualization.

Schwartz, Tony, and Jim Loehr. *The Power of Full Engagement.* New York: The Free Press, 2003. Beautifully written guide to high performance and personal fulfillment.

Seligman, Martin. *Learned Optimism.* New York: Pocket Books, 1991. The optimist's handbook.

Senge, Peter M. *The Fifth Discipline: The Art & Practice of the Learn-*

ing Organization. New York: Doubleday, 1990. An organizational guide to learning how to learn.

Summers, Kit. *Juggling with Finesse.* San Diego: Finesse Press, 1987. A compendium of jugglerian models of excellence.

Sutton, Robert. *Weird Ideas That Work.* New York: The Free Press, 2002. A compelling, lively, and practical guide for innovators.

Sluyter, Dean. *Why the Chicken Crossed the Road and Other Hidden Enlightenment Teachings.* New York: Penguin Putnam, 1998. Enlightenment made easy.

Von Oech, Roger. *A Whack on the Side of the Head,* revised ed. New York: Warner Books, 1990. Von Oech celebrates the power of play to unleash the creative process.

INDEX

Index

Index

Index

ABOUT THE AUTHOR

Michael J. Gelb is a globally acclaimed pioneer in the fields of accelerated learning, creative thinking, and leadership development. He is the president of High Performance Learning, an international management training, consulting, and executive coaching firm based in the New York metropolitan area. Established in 1977, HPL counts among its clients corporate giants including AMEC, BP, DuPont, KPMG, Merck, Microsoft, Nike, and Western Union. Michael Gelb is the author of the *New York Times* business best-seller *How to Think Like Leonardo da Vinci,* which has been translated into eighteen languages. Gelb is also the author of *The New Mind Map, Present Yourself: Captivate Your Audience with Great Presentations, Thinking for a Change,* and *Discover Your Genius: How to Think Like History's Ten Most Revolutionary Minds.* A third-degree black belt in the martial art of Aikido, Gelb is coauthor with chess Grandmaster Raymond Keene of *Samurai Chess: Mastering Strategy Through the Martial Art of the Mind.* Michael Gelb's first book, *BodyLearning: An Introduction to the Alexander Technique,* debuted in 1981 and has become the standard text in the field.

Michael Gelb's work has been featured in *The New York Times,* the *London Review of Books, Executive Excellence,* the *Washington Post, USA Today, Investor's Business Daily, Industry Week,* and many other publications. He has juggled live on *Good Morning America* and appeared on many other television and radio programs including *Talk of the Nation, The Diane Rehm Show,* and *The Connection.* Gelb was the corecipient, with former senator John Glenn, of the 1999 Brain Foundation "Brain of the Year" Award (previous winners include Stephen Hawking, Bill Gates, Garry Kasparov, and Gene Roddenberry). In 2002, Gelb was awarded a Batten Fellowship by the University of Virginia's Darden Graduate School of Business. He has also lectured for George Mason University's Executive MBA program and at the University of Pennsylvania's Wharton School.